CiscoNet
Solutions

Copyright Notice

CCNA v3 Lab Guide: Routing and Switching 200-125

Copyright 2017 CiscoNet Solutions All Rights Reserved

Contents

Part 5: Network Troubleshooting

Introduction

Cisco CCNA certification has become increasingly complex with both theoretical and lab oriented questions. The candidate must answer technical questions and have the skills required to configure, verify and troubleshoot network connectivity. This lab guide provides CCNA v3 candidates with the skills necessary to pass CCNA simlet questions. There are 44 labs that start from the most basic global configuration to complex troubleshooting.

There are switching, routing and IPv6 addressing sections all based on CCNA v3 exam guidelines. The troubleshooting skills are a key aspect of the CCNA v3 exam covered with the lab guide. The candidate will learn a standard troubleshooting methodology required for CCNA style questions. The step-by-step format includes analysis and resolution of switching, routing, WAN, security and device management issues. The lab guide is based on the book *CCNA v3 Routing and Switching 200-125*.

Packet Tracer Fundamentals

What is Cisco Packet Tracer?

Packet Tracer is a network simulator available from Cisco that provides a virtual lab environment for CCNA candidates. The network simulator enables the candidate to configure, verify and troubleshoot network designs based on Cisco devices. Packet Tracer simulates the same IOS software and configuration as the physical devices. The labs included with this lab guide are based on official Cisco CCNA v3 exam guidelines.

Download Packet Tracer

Cisco now provides a link to download Packet Tracer that is available with the free one hour course on Packet Tracer fundamentals. The free course is available at the following link and required for the lab guide. https://www.netacad.com/campaign/ptdt-1/

Starting Labs

There are 44 Packet Tracer files (.pkt) included that are referenced by name in the lab guide with each individual lab. Start the lab by double-clicking the filename referenced for that lab.

- Start with Lab 1-1 and do the labs consecutively as they are ordered with the lab workbook.
- Follow the steps provided in the lab for configuring, verifying and/or troubleshooting.
- Exit from the lab and proceed to the next lab in the guide.

Packet Tracer Usage

The network devices all power-up when starting any Packet Tracer lab as part of the simulated lab environment. Each device on the topology is selected with a single click only. That will open a menu on routers and switches that allow configuration (CLI folder). The Physical folder allows for adding new hardware and restarting the device. The host folders are somewhat different where there is access to a command prompt and application services.

Select device icon (one click)
- *CLI* Folder – IOS configuration
- *Physical* Folder – restart devices

Select host icon (one click)
- *Config* folder
  - Global settings - IPv4/IPv6 gateway address, DHCP
  - FastEthernet0 - static IP address and subnet mask
- *Desktop* folder – command prompt (Ping, Tracert, Telnet, SSH) web browser

Lab Conventions

- IOS commands to type are bolded
- Any keys are noted with brackets <enter>
- Expected results from Ping are noted

Additional Notes

The following are some additional notes for Packet Tracer usage:

- Wait for 10 seconds after stating any lab for devices to power up.
    - Select Fast Forward Time after doing the following activities:
    - Power cycle all devices
    - Restarted device from off/on power switch
    - Any reload from the CLI

- The expected result for any ping test is indicated in with yes/no. Sometimes network convergence issues cause some ping drops so retry **ping** when there is less than 100%.

- Type exit to return from remote Telnet or SSH session.

- The return key <enter> is required twice after some IOS commands including **end**, **no shutdown** and **copy running-config startup-config**.

- The switch and router interfaces such as fastethernet0/0 for instance can be typed as Fa0/0. In addition **copy running-config startup-config** can be typed as **copy run start.**

- The IOS command **show running-config** can be typed as **show run**.

- Packet Tracer simulates the same IOS software and configuration as the physical devices. Most labs when started will arrive at a message - *press RETURN to get started.* Hit the <enter> to arrive at user mode prompt (router >).

- Type enable, hit <enter> key and when required type any password when starting devices based on lab instructions. device > **enable**

- Resize the CLI window to the right when the results for show commands are not aligned.

- Make a backup copy of the lab guide package including packet tracer files.

- Email ccna@cisconetsolutions.com should you have any additional questions or concerns.

Download Packet Tracer labs from the following location:

http://www.cisconetsolutions.com/ccnav3labs.zip

1.0 Initial Device Configuration

Lab 1-1: Global Commands

Lab Summary: The global configuration commands are the same for Cisco switches and routers deployed with similar versions of IOS code. The following are standard global commands typically configured on all Cisco switches and routers.

Figure 1-1 Lab Topology

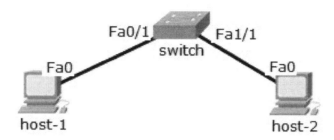

Lab Configuration

Start Packet Tracer File: **Lab 1-1 Global Commands**

Step 1: Click *Switch* icon and select the *CLI* folder. Press <enter> key for user mode prompt.

Step 2: From the user mode prompt (>) type **enable** and press <enter> key.

Step 3: From the enable mode prompt type the following to start configuring the switch.

      switch# **configure terminal** <enter>

Step 4: Configure the following global IOS commands on the switch:

      switch(config)# **hostname switch-1** <enter>
      switch-1(config)# **service password-encryption** <enter>
      switch-1(config)# **enable password cisconet** <enter>
      switch-1(config)# **ip domain-name lab.cisconet.com** <enter>
      switch-1(config)# **ip name-server 192.168.3.3** <enter>
      switch-1(config)# **ip domain-lookup** <enter>
      switch-1(config)# **service timestamps log datetime msec** <enter>
      switch-1(config)# **clock timezone PST -8** <enter>
      switch-1(config)# **banner motd ^** <enter> **Unauthorized access not allowed ^** <enter>
      switch-1(config)# **end** <enter> and <enter>

Step 5: Save the running configuration to the startup configuration file

      switch-1# **copy running-config startup-config** <enter> <enter>

Step 6: Verify the configuration is correct and hit the spacebar repeatedly until you reach the bottom of the script and return to enable mode prompt.

switch-1# **show running-config** <enter> then three <spacebar>

Step 7: Verify the current IOS version and feature set license installed on the switch:

switch-1# **show version** <enter> then <spacebar> <spacebar>

Lab 1-2: System Management

Lab Summary: Configure and verify basic system management access for switches and routers. In addition enable SNMP community strings and standard logging to a Syslog server.

Figure 1-2 Lab Topology

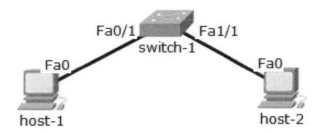

Lab Configuration:

Start Packet Tracer File: **Lab 1-2 System Management**

Step 1: Click *Switch-1* icon and select the *CLI* folder. Press <enter> key for user mode prompt.

Step 2: Enable login to the local console port with password *ccnalab:*.

> switch-1> **enable** <enter>
> password: **cisconet** <enter>
> switch-1# **configure terminal** <enter>
> switch-1(config)# **line con 0** <enter>
> switch-1(config-line)# **password ccnalab** <enter>
> switch-1(config-line)# **login** <enter>

Step 3: Configure Telnet remote access with password *ccnalab* and timeout 5 minutes.

> switch-1(config-line)# **line vty 0 4** <enter>
> switch-1(config-line)# **password ccnaexam** <enter>
> switch-1(config-line)# **login** <enter>
> switch-1(config-line)# **exec-timeout 5** <enter>
> switch-1(config-line)# **exit** <enter>

Step 4: Configure SNMP community strings

> switch-1(config)# **snmp-server community cisco ro** <enter>
> switch-1(config)# **snmp-server community ccnacourse rw** <enter>

Step 5: Enable logging and send messages to a Syslog server

> switch-1(config)# **logging on** <enter>
> switch-1(config)# **logging host 192.168.3.1** <enter>
> switch-1(config)# **end** <enter> <enter>

Step 6: Copy the running configuration to the startup configuration file:

switch-1# **copy running-config startup-config** <enter> <enter>

Step 7: Verify the initial device configuration is correct:

switch-1# **show running-config** <enter>

2.0 LAN Switching Technologies

Lab 2-1: Device Security

Lab Summary: Configure and verify basic device security features to routers and switches with password encryption and local authentication.

Figure 2-1 Lab Topology

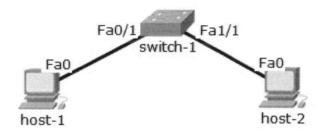

Lab Configuration

Start Packet Tracer File: **Lab 2-1 Device Security**

Step 1: Click *Switch-1* icon and select the *CLI* folder. Press <enter> key for user mode prompt.

Step 2: Enter global configuration mode

> switch-1 > **enable** <enter>
> switch-1# **configure terminal** <enter>

Step 3: Enable global password encryption

> switch-1(config)# **service password-encryption** <enter>

Step 4: Configure an enable password *ccnalabexam* with optimized MD5 encryption

> switch-1(config)# **enable secret ccnaexam** <enter>
> switch-1(config)# **exit** <enter> <enter>
> switch-1# **show running-config** <enter>

> highlight encrypted password from line - *enable secret 5 [encrypted password]* and click copy. Hit spacebar until enable mode prompt appears.

> switch-1# **configure terminal** <enter>
> switch-1(config)# **enable secret 5** <space> [click paste] <enter>

Step 5: Configure local username cisco with privilege level 15 and encrypted password ccnalabs

> switch-1(config)# **username cisco privilege 15 password ccnalabs** <enter>
> switch-1(config)# **end** <enter> <enter>
> switch-1# **show running-config** <enter>

highlight encrypted password from line - *username cisco privilege 15 password 7 [encrypted password]* and click copy. Hit spacebar until enable mode prompt appears.

switch-1# **configure terminal** <enter>
switch-1(config)# **username cisco privilege 15 password 7** <space> [click paste] <enter>
switch-1(config)# **end** <enter>

Step 6: Verify the device security configuration is correct

switch-1# **show running-config** <enter>

Lab 2-2: VLANs

Lab Summary: Configure VLANs on switch-1 with assigned names and verify the VLANs are active.

Figure 2-2 Lab Topology

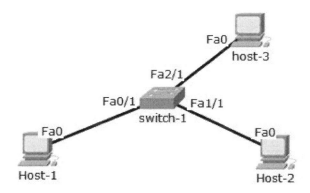

Lab Configuration

Start Packet Tracer File: **Lab 2-2 VLANS**

Click on the *switch-1* icon and select the *CLI* folder. Hit the <enter> key for user mode prompt (>).

Step 1: Enter global configuration mode

> switch> **enable** <enter>
> Password: **cisconet** <enter>
> switch# **configure terminal** <enter>

Step 2: Create the following VLANs and assign names

> switch-1(config)# **vlan 9** <enter>
> switch-1(config-vlan)# **name data** <enter>
> switch-1(config-vlan)# **vlan 10** <enter>
> switch-1(config-vlan)# **name voice** <enter>
> switch-1(config-vlan)# **vlan 11** <enter>
> switch-1(config-vlan)# **name server** <enter>
> switch-1(config-vlan)# **vlan 12** <enter>
> switch-1(config-vlan)# **name wireless** <enter>
> switch-1(config-vlan)# **exit** <enter>
> switch-1(config)# **vtp mode transparent** <enter>
> switch-1(config)# **end** <enter>
> switch-1# **copy running-config startup-config** <enter>

Step 3: Verify the VLANs are created, showing as active and no switch ports are assigned yet:

> switch-1# **show running-config** <enter>
>
> switch-1# **show vlan brief**<enter>

Lab 2-3: Access Ports

Lab Summary: Configure switch interfaces as access type ports and assign VLANs.

Figure 2-3 Lab Topology

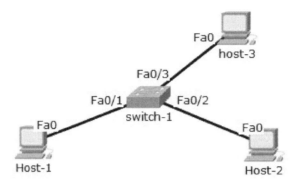

Lab Configuration

Start Packet Tracer File: **Lab 2-3 Access Ports**

Click on the *switch-1* icon and select the *CLI* folder. Hit the <enter> key for user mode prompt (>).

Step 1: Enter global configuration mode

     switch-1> **enable** <enter>
     Password: **cisconet** <enter>
     switch-1# **configure terminal** <enter>

Step 2: Configure interface Fa0/1 as an access port and assign it to VLAN 9

     switch-1(config)# **interface fastethernet0/1** <enter>
     switch-1(config-if)# **switchport mode access** <enter>
     switch-1(config-if)# **switchport access vlan 9** <enter>

Step 3: Configure interface Fa0/2 as an access port and assign it to VLAN 10

     switch-1(config-if)# **interface fastethernet 0/2** <enter>
     switch-1(config-if)# **switchport mode access** <enter>
     switch-1(config-if)# **switchport access vlan 10** <enter>

Step 4: Configure interface Fa0/3 as an access port and assign it to VLAN 11

     switch-1(config-if)# **interface fastethernet 0/3** <enter>
     switch-1(config-if)# **switchport mode access** <enter>
     switch-1(config-if)# **switchport access vlan 11** <enter>

Step 5: Configure interface range Fa0/4-24 as access ports and assign to VLAN 12

switch-1(config-if)# **interface range fastethernet0/4-24** <enter>
switch-1(config-if)# **switchport mode access** <enter>
switch-1(config-if)# **switchport access vlan 12** <enter>
switch-1(config-if)# **end** <enter>
switch-1# **copy running-config startup-config** <enter>

Step 6: Verify Lab

Verify switch access ports, interface status and VLAN assignment:

switch-1# **show running-config** <enter>

switch-1# **show vlan brief** <enter>

VLAN Name	Status	Ports
1 default	active	Gig0/1, Gig0/2
9 VLAN0009	active	Fa0/1
10 VLAN0010	active	Fa0/2
11 VLAN0011	active	Fa0/3
12 VLAN0012	active	Fa0/4, Fa0/5, Fa0/6, Fa0/7
		Fa0/8, Fa0/9, Fa0/10, Fa0/11
		Fa0/12, Fa0/13, Fa0/14, Fa0/15
		Fa0/16, Fa0/17, Fa0/18, Fa0/19
		Fa0/20, Fa0/21, Fa0/22, Fa0/23
		Fa0/24
1002 fddi-default	active	
1003 token-ring-default	active	
1004 fddinet-default	active	
1005 trnet-default	active	

switch-1# **show vlan** <enter>

Lab Notes

The range keyword allows you to apply the configuration to multiple switch ports with a single command. The range keyword is omitted and a single interface is specified when configuring IOS commands on a single interface.

Lab 2-4 Switch Management

Lab Summary: Configure switch-1 to allow remote management access from a Telnet session.

Figure 2-4 Lab Topology

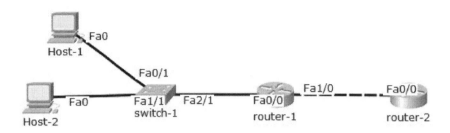

Lab Configuration

Start Packet Tracer File: **Lab 2-4 Switch Management**

Click on the *switch-1* icon and select the *CLI* folder. Hit the <enter> key for user mode prompt (>).

Step 1: Enter global configuration mode

switch-1> **enable** <enter>
switch-1# **configure terminal** <enter>

Step 2: Configure VLAN 10 SVI for switch management

switch-1(config)# **interface vlan 10** <enter>
switch-1(config-if)# **description switch management** <enter>
switch-1(config-if)# **ip address 192.168.1.254 255.255.255.0** <enter>
switch-1(config-if)# **no shutdown** <enter>
switch-1(config-if)# **exit** <enter>

Step 3: Configure the default gateway address

switch-1(config)# **ip default-gateway 192.168.1.3** <enter>

Step 4: Configure VTY lines 0 4 for remote management access

switch-1(config)# **enable password cisconet** <enter>
switch-1(config)# **line vty 0 4** <enter>
switch-1(config-line)# **password cisco** <enter>
switch-1(config-line)# **login** <enter>
switch-1(config-line)# **end** <enter>
switch-1# **copy running-config startup-config** <enter>

Step 5: <u>Verify Lab</u>

Verify the configuration is correct on switch-1 and confirm VLAN 10 (192.168.1.254/24) interface is operational (up/up) on switch-1. Start a Telnet session from each router to switch-1 and verify there is remote access.

       switch-1# **show running-config** <enter>
       switch-1# **show ip interface brief** <enter>

       router-1# **telnet 192.168.1.254** <enter>
       password: **cisco** <enter>
       switch-1 > **enable** <enter>
       password: **cisconet** <enter>
       switch-1# **exit** <enter>

       router-2# **telnet 192.168.1.254** <enter>
       password: **cisco** <enter>
       switch-1 > **enable** <enter>
       password: **cisconet** <enter>
       switch-1# **exit** <enter>

<u>Lab Notes:</u>

The **ip default-gateway** command is required on switch-1 to allow Telnet access from any device not on the local subnet such as router-2.

Lab 2-5 Port Security

Lab Summary: Enable port security on switch ports and maximum number of connections feature.

Figure 2-5 Lab Topology

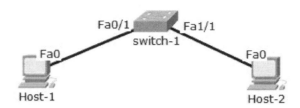

Lab Configuration

Start Packet Tracer File: **Lab 2-5 Port Security**

Click on the *switch-1* icon and select the *CLI* folder. Hit the <enter> key for user mode prompt (>).

Step 1: Enter global configuration mode

> switch-1> **enable** <enter>
> Password: **cisconet** <enter>
> switch-1# **configure terminal** <enter>

Step 2: Enable port security on switch port Fa0/1 (host-1)

> switch-1(config)# **interface fastethernet0/1** <enter>
> switch-1(config-if)# **switchport mode access** <enter>
> switch-1(config-if)# **switchport access vlan 10** <enter>
> switch-1(config-if)# **switchport port-security** <enter>
> switch-1(config-if)# **switchport port-security mac-address sticky** <enter>

Step 3: Enable port security on switch port Fa1/1 (host-2)

> switch-1(config)# **interface fastethernet1/1** <enter>
> switch-1(config-if)# **switchport mode access** <enter>
> switch-1(config-if)# **switchport access vlan 10** <enter>
> switch-1(config-if)# **switchport port-security** <enter>
> switch-1(config-if)# **switchport port-security mac-address sticky** <enter>

Step 4: Configure a maximum of 2 connections permitted on interface Fa0/1 (host-1)

> switch-1(config)# **interface fastethernet0/1** <enter>
> switch-1(config-if)# **switchport port-security maximum 2** <enter>
> switch-1(config-if)# **end** <enter>
> switch-1# **copy running-config startup-config** <enter>

Step 5: Verify Lab

Verify port security configuration and operational status for host-1 and host-2:

switch-1# **show running-config** <enter>

switch-1# **show port-security interface fastethernet0/1** <enter>

Port Security	**: Enabled**
Port Status	**: Secure-up**
Violation Mode	: Shutdown
Aging Time	: 0 mins
Aging Type	: Absolute
SecureStatic Address Aging	: Disabled
Maximum MAC Addresses	**: 2**
Total MAC Addresses	: 0
Configured MAC Addresses	: 0
Sticky MAC Addresses	: 0
Last Source Address:Vlan	: 0000.0000.0000:0
Security Violation Count	: 0

switch-1# **show port-security interface fastethernet1/1** <enter>

Port Security	**: Enabled**
Port Status	**: Secure-up**
Violation Mode	: Shutdown
Aging Time	: 0 mins
Aging Type	: Absolute
SecureStatic Address Aging	: Disabled
Maximum MAC Addresses	**: 1**
Total MAC Addresses	: 0
Configured MAC Addresses	: 0
Sticky MAC Addresses	: 0
Last Source Address:Vlan	: 0000.0000.0000:0
Security Violation Count	: 0

Lab 2-6 Static Trunking

Lab Summary: Configure access ports, assign VLANs and enable trunking between the switches.

Figure 2-6 Lab Topology

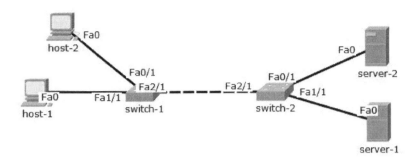

Lab Configuration

Start Packet Tracer File: **Lab 2-6 Static Trunking**

Switch-1:

Click on the *switch-1* icon and select the *CLI* folder. Hit the <enter> key for user mode prompt (>).

Step 1: Enter global configuration mode

> switch-1> **enable** <enter>
> Password: **cisconet** <enter>
> switch-1# **configure terminal** <enter>

Step 2: Create VLAN 10 and assign it to interface Fa0/1

> switch-1(config)# **vlan 10** <enter>
> switch-1(config-vlan)# **exit** <enter>
> switch-1(config)# **interface fastethernet0/1** <enter>
> switch-1(config-if)# **switchport mode access** <enter>
> switch-1(config-if)# **switchport access vlan 10** <enter>
> switch-1(config-if)# **exit** <enter>

Step 3: Create VLAN 11 and assign it to interface Fa1/1

> switch-1(config)# **vlan 11** <enter>
> switch-1(config-vlan)# **exit** <enter>
> switch-1(config)# **interface fastethernet1/1** <enter>
> switch-1(config-if)# **switchport mode access** <enter>
> switch-1(config-if)# **switchport access vlan 11** <enter>
> switch-1(config-if)# **exit** <enter>

Step 4: Enable Fastethernet2/1 as a trunk interface and turn off DTP negotiation

      switch-1(config)# **interface fastethernet2/1** <enter>
      switch-1(config-if)# **switchport mode trunk** <enter>
      switch-1(config-if)# **switchport nonegotiate** <enter>

Step 5: Change the native VLAN to 999 and allow only VLAN 10 and 11 across the trunk.

      switch-1(config-if)# **switchport trunk native vlan 999** <enter>
      switch-1(config-if)# **switchport trunk allowed vlan 10,11** <enter>
      switch-1(config-if)# **end** <enter>
      switch-1# **copy running-config startup-config** <enter>

Switch-2:

Click on the *switch-2* icon and select the *CLI* folder. Hit the <enter> key for user mode prompt (>).

Step 6: Enter global configuration mode

      switch-2> **enable** <enter>
      Password: **cisconet** <enter>
      switch-2# **configure terminal** <enter>

Step 7: Create VLAN 10 and assign it to interface Fa0/1

      switch-2(config)# **vlan 10** <enter>
      switch-2(config-vlan)# **exit** <enter>
      switch-2(config)# **interface fastethernet0/1** <enter>
      switch-2(config-if)# **switchport mode access** <enter>
      switch-2(config-if)# **switchport access vlan 10** <enter>
      switch-2(config-if)# **exit** <enter>

Step 8: Create VLAN 11 and assign it to interface Fa1/1

      switch-2(config)# **vlan 11** <enter>
      switch-2(config-vlan)# **exit** <enter>
      switch-2(config)# **interface fastethernet1/1** <enter>
      switch-2(config-if)# **switchport mode access** <enter>
      switch-2(config-if)# **switchport access vlan 11** <enter>
      switch-2(config-if)# **exit** <enter>

Step 9: Enable Fastethernet2/1 as a trunk interface and turn off DTP negotiation

      switch-2(config)# **interface fastethernet2/1** <enter>
      switch-2(config-if)# **switchport mode trunk** <enter>
      switch-2(config-if)# **switchport nonegotiate** <enter>

Step 10: Change the native VLAN to 999 and allow only VLAN 10 and 11 across the trunk link.

switch-2(config-if)# **switchport trunk native vlan 999** <enter>

switch-2(config-if)# **switchport trunk allowed vlan 10,11** <enter>

switch-2(config-if)# **end** <enter>

switch-2# **copy running-config startup-config** <enter>

Step 11: Verify Lab

Verify the lab configuration is correct and confirm trunking is operational for interface Fa2/1 of both switches and the native VLAN is 999. In addition confirm VLAN 10 and VLAN 11 are allowed across the trunk interface. Verify host-1 can ping server-1 in the same subnet (192.168.1.2/24) and not server-2 (192.168.2.2/24). Verify as well that host-2 can ping server-2 and not server-1.

switch-1# **show running-config** <enter>

switch-2# **show running-config** <enter>

switch-1# **show interfaces trunk**<enter>

Port	Mode	Encapsulation	Status	Native vlan
Fa2/1	on	802.1q	trunking	999

Port	Vlans allowed on trunk
Fa2/1	10-11

Port	Vlans allowed and active in management domain
Fa2/1	10,11

Port	Vlans in spanning tree forwarding state and not pruned
Fa2/1	none

switch-2# **show interfaces trunk**<enter>

host-1: **c:\>ping 192.168.1.2** <enter> **(yes)**

host-1: **c:\>ping 192.168.2.2** <enter> **(no)**

host-2: **c:\>ping 192.168.2.2** <enter> **(yes)**

host-2: **c:\>ping 192.168.1.2** <enter> **(no)**

Lab Notes

The purpose of Dynamic Trunking Protocol (DTP) is to automatically negotiate trunking between neighbor switches. The default for Cisco switches is DTP enabled and trunk interfaces are enabled based on switch interface configuration. The **switchport mode trunk** command configures a static trunk with **on** mode (manual). The **switchport nonegotiate** command turns off DTP as a recommended security best practice for static trunks.

Lab 2-7 Layer 2 EtherChannel

Lab Summary: Configure EtherChannel port aggregation between switch-1 and switch-2 with PAgP
negotiation. In addition assign the bundle to a port channel interface and verify the lab.

Figure 2-7 Lab Topology

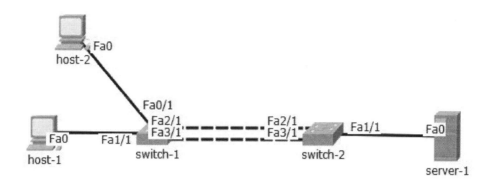

Lab Configuration:

Start Packet Tracer File: **Lab 2-7 EtherChannel**

Switch-1

Click on the *switch-1* icon and select the *CLI* folder. Hit the <enter> key for user mode prompt (>).

Step 1: Enter global configuration mode

    switch-1> **enable** <enter>
    Password: **cisconet** <enter>
    switch-1# **configure terminal** <enter>

Step 2: Configure interface Fa0/1 as an access port and assign it to VLAN 12:

    switch-1(config)# **vlan 12** <enter>
    switch-1(config-vlan)# **exit** <enter>
    switch-1(config)# **interface fastethernet0/1** <enter>
    switch-1(config-if)# **switchport mode access** <enter>
    switch-1(config-if)# **switchport access vlan 12** <enter>
    switch-1(config-if)# **exit** <enter>

Step 3: Configure interface Fa1/1 as an access port and assign it to VLAN 12:

    switch-1(config)# **interface fastethernet1/1** <enter>
    switch-1(config-if)# **switchport mode access** <enter>
    switch-1(config-if)# **switchport access vlan 12** <enter>
    switch-1(config-if)# **exit** <enter>

Step 4: Add FastEthernet2/1 to EtherChannel with PAgP desirable mode and assign channel group 1.

```
switch-1(config)# interface fastethernet2/1 <enter>
switch-1(config-if)# switchport mode trunk <enter>
switch-1(config-if)# channel-group 1 mode desirable <enter>
switch-1(config-if)# no shutdown <enter>
switch-1(config-if)# exit <enter>
```

Step 5: Add FastEthernet3/1 to EtherChannel with PAgP desirable mode and assign channel group 1.

```
switch-1(config)# interface fastethernet3/1 <enter>
switch-1(config-if)# switchport mode trunk <enter>
switch-1(config-if)# channel-group 1 mode desirable <enter>
switch-1(config-if)# no shutdown <enter>
switch-1(config-if)# exit <enter>
```

Step 6: Enable interface port channel 1 (Po1) for channel-group 1

```
switch-1(config)# interface port-channel1 <enter>
switch-1(config-if)# switchport mode trunk <enter>
switch-1(config-if)# no shutdown <enter>
switch-1(config-if)# end <enter>
switch-1# copy running-config startup-config <enter>
```

Switch-2:

Click on the *switch-2* icon and select the *CLI* folder. Hit the <enter> key for user mode prompt (>).

Step 7: Enter global configuration mode

```
switch-2> enable <enter>
Password: cisconet <enter>
switch-2# configure terminal <enter>
```

Step 8: Configure Fa0/1 as an access port and assign it to VLAN 12:

```
switch-2(config)# vlan 12 <enter>
switch-2(config-vlan)# exit <enter>
switch-2(config)# interface fastethernet0/1 <enter>
switch-2(config-if)# switchport mode access <enter>
switch-2(config-if)# switchport access vlan 12 <enter>
switch-2(config-if)# exit <enter>
```

Step 9: Configure Fa1/1 as an access port and assign it to VLAN 12:
```
switch-2(config)# interface fastethernet1/1 <enter>
switch-2(config-if)# switchport mode access <enter>
switch-2(config-if)# switchport access vlan 12 <enter>
switch-2(config-if)# exit <enter>
```

Step 10: Add FastEthernet2/1 to EtherChannel with PAgP desirable mode and assign channel group 1:

    switch-2(config)# **interface fastethernet2/1** <enter>
    switch-2(config-if)# **switchport mode trunk** <enter>
    switch-2(config-if)# **channel-group 1 mode desirable** <enter>
    switch-2(config-if)# **no shutdown** <enter>
    switch-(config-if)# **exit** <enter>

Step 11: Add FastEthernet3/1 to EtherChannel with PAgP desirable mode and assign channel group 1:

    switch-2(config)# **interface fastethernet3/1** <enter>
    switch-2(config-if)# **switchport mode trunk** <enter>
    switch-2(config-if)# **channel-group 1 mode desirable** <enter>
    switch-2(config-if)# **no shutdown** <enter>
    switch-2(config-if)# **exit** <enter>

Step 12: Enable interface port channel 1 (Po1) for channel-group 1

    switch-2(config)# **interface port-channel1** <enter>
    switch-2(config-if)# **switchport mode trunk** <enter>
    switch-2(config-if)# **no shutdown** <enter>
    switch-2(config-if)# **end** <enter>
    switch-2# **copy running-config startup-config** <enter>

Step 13: Verify Lab

Verify EtherChannel configuration, operational status and neighbor connectivity:

    switch-1# **show running-config** <enter>

    switch-1# **show cdp neighbors** <enter>

Device ID	Local Intrfce	Holdtme	Capability	Platform	Port ID
switch-2	Fas 2/1	154	S	PT3000	Fas 2/1
switch-2	Fas 3/1	154	S	PT3000	Fas 3/1

    switch-1# **show etherchannel summary** <enter>

Number of channel-groups in use: 1
Number of aggregators: 1

Group Port-channel Protocol Ports
----

1 Po1(SU) PAgP Fa2/1(P) Fa3/1(P)

Lab Notes

Etherchannel creates a single logical channel (bundle) comprised of Fa2/1 and Fa3/1 on both switches. The port channel assigns a single logical interface to that bundle. The channel group number is linked to the port channel interface number for that purpose.

Lab 2-8: Rapid STP (RSTP)

Lab Summary: Configure access ports and assign VLANs to switch-1 and switch-2. In addition provide layer 2 connectivity between the switches with a trunk and enable RPVST+.

Figure 2-8 Lab Topology

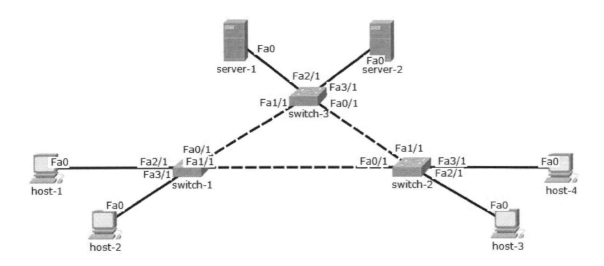

Lab Configuration

Start Packet Tracer File: **Lab 2-8 Rapid STP**

Switch 1:

Click on the *switch-1* icon and select the *CLI* folder. Hit the <enter> key for user mode prompt (>).

Step 1: Enter global configuration mode

     switch-1> **enable** <enter>
     Password: **cisconet** <enter>
     switch-1# **configure terminal** <enter>

Step 2: Create VLAN 10 and VLAN 11

     switch-1(config)# **vlan 10** <enter>
     switch-1(config-vlan)# **vlan 11** <enter>
     switch-1(config-vlan)# **exit** <enter>

Step 3: Configure interface Fa2/1 as an access port and assign to VLAN 10

     switch-1(config)# **interface fastethernet2/1** <enter>
     switch-1(config-if)# **switchport mode access** <enter>
     switch-1(config-if)# **switchport access vlan 10** <enter>
     switch-1(config-if)# **exit** <enter>

Step 4: Configure interface Fa3/1 as an access port and assign to VLAN 11

    switch-1(config)# **interface fastethernet3/1** <enter>
    switch-1(config-if)# **switchport mode access** <enter>
    switch-1(config-if)# **switchport access vlan 11** <enter>
    switch-1(config-if)# **exit** <enter>

Step 5: Assign Fa0/1 as a trunk interface and allow VLAN 10 and VLAN 11

    switch-1(config)# **interface fastethernet0/1** <enter>
    switch-1(config-if)# **switchport mode trunk** <enter>
    switch-1(config-if)# **switchport trunk allowed vlan 10-11** <enter>
    switch-1(config-if)# **exit** <enter>

Step 6: Assign Fa1/1 as a trunk interface and allow VLAN 10 and VLAN 11

    switch-1(config)# **interface fastethernet1/1** <enter>
    switch-1(config-if)# **switchport mode trunk** <enter>
    switch-1(config-if)# **switchport trunk allowed vlan 10-11** <enter>
    switch-1(config-if)# **exit** <enter>

Step 7: Enable Rapid Per VLAN Spanning Tree Protocol (RPVST+)

    switch-1(config)# **spanning-tree mode rapid-pvst** <enter>
    switch-1(config)# **end** <enter>
    switch-1# **copy running-config startup-config** <enter>

Switch-2:

Click on the *switch-2* icon and select the *CLI* folder. Hit the <enter> key for user mode prompt (>).

Step 8: Enter global configuration mode

    switch-2> **enable** <enter>
    Password: **cisconet** <enter>
    switch-2# **configure terminal** <enter>

Step 9: Create VLAN 10 and VLAN 11

    switch-2(config)# **vlan 10** <enter>
    switch-2(config-vlan)# **vlan 11** <enter>
    switch-2(config-vlan)# **exit** <enter>

Step 10: Configure interface Fa2/1 as an access port and assign to VLAN 10

    switch-2(config)# **interface fastethernet2/1** <enter>
    switch-2(config-if)# **switchport mode access** <enter>
    switch-2(config-if)# **switchport access vlan 10** <enter>
    switch-2(config-if)# **exit** <enter>

Step 11: Configure interface Fa3/1 as an access port and assign to VLAN 11

    switch-2(config)# **interface fastethernet3/1** <enter>
    switch-2(config-if)# **switchport mode access** <enter>
    switch-2(config-if)# **switchport access vlan 11** <enter>
    switch-2(config-if)# **exit** <enter>

Step 12: Assign Fa0/1 as a trunk interface and assign to VLAN 10

    switch-2(config)# **interface fastethernet0/1** <enter>
    switch-2(config-if)# **switchport mode trunk** <enter>
    switch-2(config-if)# **switchport trunk allowed vlan 10-11** <enter>
    switch-2(config-if)# **exit** <enter>

Step 13 :Assign Fa1/1 as a trunk interface and assign to VLAN 11

    switch-2(config)# **interface fastethernet1/1** <enter>
    switch-2(config-if)# **switchport mode trunk** <enter>
    switch-2(config-if)# **switchport trunk allowed vlan 10-11** <enter>
    switch-2(config-if)# **exit** <enter>

Step 14: Enable Rapid Per VLAN Spanning Tree Protocol (RPVST+)

    switch-2(config)# **spanning-tree mode rapid-pvst** <enter>
    switch-2(config)# **end** <enter>
    switch-2# **copy running-config startup-config** <enter>

Switch-3:

Click on the *switch-3* icon and select the *CLI* folder. Hit the <enter> key for user mode prompt (>).

Step 15: Enter global configuration mode

    switch-3> **enable** <enter>
    Password: **cisconet** <enter>
    switch-3# **configure terminal** <enter>

Step 16: Create VLAN 10 and VLAN 11

    switch-3(config)# **vlan 10** <enter>
    switch-3(config-vlan)# **vlan 11** <enter>
    switch-3(config-vlan)# **exit** <enter>

Step 17: Configure interface Fa2/1 as an access port and assign to VLAN 10

    switch-3(config)# **interface fastethernet2/1** <enter>
    switch-3(config-if)# **switchport mode access** <enter>
    switch-3(config-if)# **switchport access vlan 10** <enter>
    switch-3(config-if)# **exit** <enter>

Step 18: Configure interface Fa3/1 as an access port and assign to VLAN 11

    switch-3(config)# **interface fastethernet3/1** <enter>
    switch-3(config-if)# **switchport mode access** <enter>
    switch-3(config-if)# **switchport access vlan 11** <enter>
    switch-3(config-if)# **exit** <enter>

Step 19: Assign Fa0/1 as a trunk interface and assign to VLAN 10

    switch-3(config)# **interface fastethernet0/1** <enter>
    switch-3(config-if)# **switchport mode trunk** <enter>
    switch-3(config-if)# **switchport trunk allowed vlan 10-11** <enter>
    switch-3(config-if)# **exit** <enter>

Step 20: Assign Fa1/1 as a trunk interface and assign to VLAN 11

    switch-3(config)# **interface fastethernet1/1** <enter>
    switch-3(config-if)# **switchport mode trunk** <enter>
    switch-3(config-if)# **switchport trunk allowed vlan 10-11** <enter>
    switch-3(config-if)# **exit** <enter>

Step 21: Configure Rapid Per VLAN Spanning Tree Protocol (RPVST+)

    switch-3(config)# **spanning-tree mode rapid-pvst** <enter>
    switch-3(config)# **end** <enter>
    switch-3# **copy running-config startup-config** <enter>

Step 22: <u>Verify Lab</u>

Verify switch configurations including version, root bridge assigned and port states for VLAN 10 and 11.

    switch-1# **show running-config** <enter>

    switch-1# **show spanning-tree summary** <enter>

    switch-1# **show spanning-tree vlan 10** <enter>

    switch-1# **show spanning-tree vlan 11** <enter>

    switch-2# **show running-config** <enter>

    switch-2# **show spanning-tree summary** <enter>

    switch-2# **show spanning-tree vlan 10** <enter>

    switch-2# **show spanning-tree vlan 11** <enter>

    switch-3# **show running-config** <enter>

    switch-3# **show spanning-tree summary** <enter>

    switch-3# **show spanning-tree vlan 10** <enter>

    switch-3# **show spanning-tree vlan 11** <enter>

<u>Lab Notes:</u> The root bridge for VLAN 10 and VLAN 11 is switch-3

Lab 2-9 PortFast

Lab Summary: Configure PortFast on switch-1 access ports and verify the lab.

Figure 2-9 Lab Topology

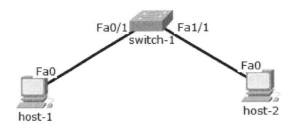

Lab Configuration

Start Packet Tracer File: **Lab 2-9 PortFast**

Click on the *switch-1* icon and select the *CLI* folder. Hit the <enter> key for user mode prompt (>).

Step 1: Enter global configuration mode

    switch-1> **enable** <enter>
    Password: **cisconet** <enter>
    switch-1# **configure terminal** <enter>

Step 2: Configure interface Fa0/1 as an access port and assign to VLAN 10

    switch-1(config)# **vlan 10** <enter>
    switch-1(config)# **interface fastethernet0/1** <enter>
    switch-1(config-if)# **switchport mode access** <enter>
    switch-1(config-if)# **switchport access vlan 10** <enter>

Step 3: Enable PortFast on interface Fa0/1

    switch-1(config-if)# **spanning-tree portfast** <enter> <enter>
    switch-1(config-if)# **exit** <enter>

Step 4: Configure interface Fa1/1 as an access port and assign to VLAN 10

    switch-1(config)# **interface fastethernet1/1** <enter>
    switch-1(config-if)# **switchport mode access** <enter>
    switch-1(config-if)# **switchport access vlan 10** <enter>

Step 5: Enable PortFast on interface Fa1/1

    switch-1(config-if)# **spanning-tree portfast** <enter> <enter>
    switch-1(config-if)# **end** <enter>
    switch-1# **copy running-config startup-config** <enter>

Step 6: <u>Verify Lab</u>

Verify the lab configuration and confirm it is enabled on Fa0/1 and Fa1/1:

> switch-1# **show running-config** <enter> <spacebar>
>
> switch-1# **show spanning-tree interface fastethernet0/1 portfast** <enter>
>
> VLAN0001   enabled
> VLAN0010   enabled
>
> switch-1# **show spanning-tree interface fastethernet1/1 portfast** <enter>

Lab 2-10: Root Bridge Selection

Lab Summary: Manually change the root bridge with the switch priority command.

Figure 2-10 Lab Topology

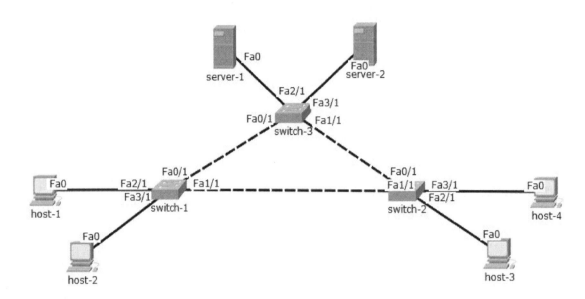

Lab Configuration

Start Packet Tracer File: **Lab 2-10 STP Root Bridge**

Click on the *switch-2* icon and select the *CLI* folder. Hit the <enter> key for user mode prompt (>).

Step 1: Enter global configuration mode

> switch-2> **enable** <enter>
> Password: **cisconet** <enter>
> switch-2#

Step 2: Verify the root bridge for VLAN 10 and VLAN 11 is switch-2 (resize box to the right)

> switch-2# **show spanning-tree vlan 10** <enter>
> switch-2# **show spanning-tree vlan 11** <enter>

Click on the *switch-3* icon and select the *CLI* folder. Hit the <enter> key for user mode prompt (>).

Step 3: Enter global configuration mode

> switch-3> **enable** <enter>
> Password: **cisconet** <enter>
> switch-3# **configure terminal** <enter>

switch-3(config)# **spanning-tree vlan 10 priority 28672** <enter>
switch-3(config)# **spanning-tree vlan 11 priority 28672** <enter>
switch-3(config)# **end** <enter>
switch-3# **copy running-config startup-config** <enter>

Step 4: <u>Verify Lab</u>

Verify the root bridge for VLAN 10 and VLAN 11 is now switch-3 and all interfaces are designated ports.

switch-3# **show running-config** <enter>

switch-3# **show spanning-tree summary** <enter>

switch-3# **show spanning-tree vlan 10** <enter>

VLAN0010
Spanning tree enabled protocol rstp
Root ID   Priority   28682
           Address   0090.2149.B1D8
           This bridge is the root
           Hello Time 2 sec Max Age 20 sec Forward Delay 15 sec

 Bridge ID Priority   28682 (priority 28672 sys-id-ext 10)
           Address   0090.2149.B1D8
           Hello Time 2 sec Max Age 20 sec Forward Delay 15 sec
           Aging Time 20

Interface	Role	Sts	Cost	Prio.Nbr	Type
Fa0/1	Desg	FWD	19	128.1	P2p
Fa2/1	Desg	FWD	19	128.3	P2p
Fa1/1	Desg	FWD	19	128.2	P2p

switch-3# **show spanning-tree vlan 11** <enter>

VLAN0011
Spanning tree enabled protocol rstp
 Root ID   Priority   28683
           Address   0090.2149.B1D8
           This bridge is the root
           Hello Time 2 sec Max Age 20 sec Forward Delay 15 sec

Bridge ID Priority   28683 (priority 28672 sys-id-ext 11)
           Address   0090.2149.B1D8
           Hello Time 2 sec Max Age 20 sec Forward Delay 15 sec
           Aging Time 20

Interface	Role	Sts	Cost	Prio.Nbr	Type
Fa3/1	Desg	FWD	19	128.4	P2p
Fa0/1	Desg	FWD	19	128.1	P2p
Fa1/1	Desg	FWD	19	128.2	P2p

3.0 Routing Technologies

Lab 3-1: IP Addressing

Lab Summary: Configure IP addressing on the LAN/WAN interfaces of three connected routers.

Figure 3-1 Lab Topology

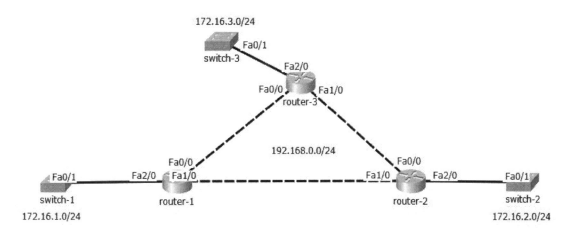

Lab Configuration

Start Packet Tracer File: **Lab 3-1 IP Addressing**

Configure the following IP address plan along with descriptions and enable the interfaces.

Hostname	Interface	IP Address	Subnet Mask	Description
router-1	Fa2/0	172.16.1.3	255.255.255.0	LAN interface
router-1	Fa1/0	192.168.1.1	255.255.255.0	router-2 link
router-1	Fa0/0	192.168.2.1	255.255.255.0	router-3 link
router-2	Fa2/0	172.16.2.3	255.255.255.0	LAN interface
router-2	Fa1/0	192.168.1.2	255.255.255.0	router-1 link
router-2	Fa0/0	192.168.16.1	255.255.255.0	router-3 link
router-3	Fa2/0	172.16.3.3	255.255.255.0	LAN interface
router-3	Fa1/0	192.168.16.2	255.255.255.0	router-2 link
router-3	Fa0/0	192.168.2.2	255.255.255.0	router-1 link

Router-1:

Click on the *router-1* icon and select the *CLI* folder. Hit the <enter> key for user mode prompt (>).

Step 1: Enter global configuration mode

      router-1> **enable** <enter>
      Password: **cisconet** <enter>
      router-1# **configure terminal** <enter>

Step 2: Configure LAN interface Fa2/0 on router-1

      router-1(config)# **interface fastethernet2/0** <enter>
      router-1(config-if)# **description LAN Interface** <enter>
      router-1(config-if)# **ip address 172.16.1.3 255.255.255.0** <enter>
      router-1(config-if)# **no shutdown** <enter>

Step 3: Configure WAN interface Fa1/0 on router-1

      router-1(config)# **interface fastethernet1/0** <enter>
      router-1(config-if)# **description router-2 link** <enter>
      router-1(config-if)# **ip address 192.168.1.1 255.255.255.0** <enter>
      router-1(config-if)# **no shutdown** <enter>

Step 4: Configure WAN interface Fa0/0 on router-1

      router-1(config)# **interface fastethernet0/0** <enter>
      router-1(config-if)# **description router-3 link** <enter>
      router-1(config-if)# **ip address 192.168.2.1 255.255.255.0** <enter>
      router-1(config-if)# **no shutdown** <enter>
      router-2(config-if)# **end** <enter>
      router-2# **copy running-config startup-config** <enter>

Router-2:

Click on the *router-2* icon and select the *CLI* folder. Hit the <enter> key for user mode prompt (>).

Step 5: Enter global configuration mode

      router-2> **enable** <enter>
      Password: **cisconet** <enter>
      router-2# **configure terminal** <enter>

Step 6: Configure LAN interface Fa2/0 on router-2

      router-2(config)# **interface fastethernet2/0** <enter>
      router-2(config-if)# **description LAN interface** <enter>
      router-2(config-if)# **ip address 172.16.2.3 255.255.255.0** <enter>
      router-2(config-if)# **no shutdown** <enter>

Step 7: Configure WAN interface Fa1/0 on router-2

    router-2(config)# **interface fastethernet1/0** <enter>
    router-2(config-if)# **description router-1 link** <enter>
    router-2(config-if)# **ip address 192.168.1.2 255.255.255.0** <enter>
    router-2(config-if)# **no shutdown** <enter>

Step 8: Configure WAN interface Fa0/0 on router-2

    router-2(config)# **interface fastethernet0/0** <enter>
    router-2(config-if)# **description router-3 link** <enter>
    router-2(config-if)# **ip address 192.168.16.1 255.255.255.0** <enter>
    router-2(config-if)# **no shutdown** <enter>
    router-2(config-if)# **end** <enter>
    router-2# **copy running-config startup-config** <enter>

Router-3:

Click on the *router-3* icon and select the *CLI* folder. Hit the <enter> key for user mode prompt (>).

Step 9: Enter global configuration mode

    router-3> **enable** <enter>
    Password: **cisconet** <enter>
    router-3# **configure terminal** <enter>

Step 10: Configure LAN interface Fa2/0 on router-3

    router-3(config)# **interface fastethernet2/0** <enter>
    router-3(config-if)# **description LAN interface** <enter>
    router-3(config-if)# **ip address 172.16.3.3 255.255.255.0** <enter>
    router-3(config-if)# **no shutdown** <enter>

Step 11: Configure WAN interface Fa1/0 on router-3

    router-3(config)# **interface fastethernet1/0** <enter>
    router-3(config-if)# **description router-2 link** <enter>
    router-3(config-if)# **ip address 192.168.16.2 255.255.255.0** <enter>
    router-3(config-if)# **no shutdown** <enter>

Step 12: Configure WAN interface Fa0/0 on router-3

    router-3(config)# **interface fastethernet0/0** <enter>
    router-3(config-if)# **description router-1 link** <enter>
    router-3(config-if)# **ip address 192.168.2.2 255.255.255.0** <enter>
    router-3(config-if)# **no shutdown** <enter>
    router-3(config-if)# **end** <enter>
    router-3# **copy running-config startup-config** <enter>

Step 13: <u>Verify Lab</u>

Verify configuration and confirm layer 3 interfaces are enabled. In addition ping the directly connected neighbor interfaces to confirm basic layer 3 connectivity.

router-1# **show running-config** <enter>

router-1# **show ip interface brief** <enter>

router-2# **show running-config** <enter>

router-2# **show ip interface brief** <enter>

router-3# **show running-config** <enter>

router-3# **show ip interface brief** <enter>

router-1# **ping 192.168.1.2** <enter>

router-1# **ping 192.168.2.2** <enter>

router-2# **ping 192.168.16.2** <enter>

<u>Lab Notes</u>

Layer 3 interfaces often require an explicit **no shutdown** command to enable packet forwarding after assigning an IP address.

Lab 3-2: Static Route

Lab Summary: Configure static routing to provide layer 3 reachability between host and server subnets.

Figure 3-2 Lab Topology

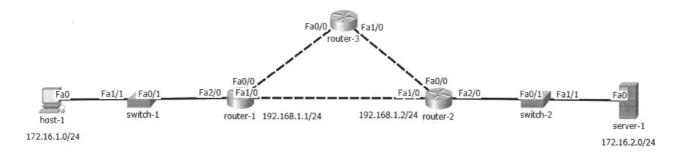

<u>Lab Configuration</u>

Start Packet Tracer File: **Lab 3-2 Static Route**

Router-1

Click on the *router-1* icon and select the *CLI* folder. Hit the <enter> key for user mode prompt (>).

Step 1: Enter global configuration mode

> router-1> **enable** <enter>
> Password: **cisconet** <enter>
> router-1# **configure terminal** <enter>

Step 2: Configure a static route on router-1 so that all packets destined for server-1 (subnet 172.16.2.0) are forwarded with 192.168.1.2 as next hop address. That is the directly connected interface of router-2

> router-1(config)# **ip route 172.16.2.0 255.255.255.0 192.168.1.2** <enter>
> router-1(config)# **end** <enter>
> router-1# **copy running-config startup-config** <enter>

Router-2

Click on the *router-2* icon and select the *CLI* folder. Hit the <enter> key for user mode prompt (>).

Step 3: Enter global configuration mode

> router-2> **enable** <enter>
> Password: **cisconet** <enter>
> router-2# **configure terminal** <enter>

Step 4: Configure a static route on router-2 so that all packets destined for subnet 172.16.1.0 (host-1) are forwarded with 192.168.1.1/24 as next hop address. That is the directly connected interface of router-1.

router-2(config)# **ip route 172.16.1.0 255.255.255.0 192.168.1.1** <enter>
router-2(config)# **end** <enter>
router-2# **copy running-config startup-config** <enter>

Step 5: Verify Lab

Verify the configuration is correct and confirm the route is installed in the routing table. In addition ping the LAN interface of router-2 to verify connectivity and routing path with traceroute command.

router-1# **show running-config** <enter>

router-1# **show ip route** <enter>

      S   172.16.2.0 [1/0] via 192.168.1.2 <enter>

router-2# **show ip route** <enter>

      S   172.16.1.0 [1/0] via 192.168.1.1 <enter>

host-1# **c:\> ping 172.16.2.1** <enter>

host-1# **c:\> tracert 172.16.2.1** <enter>

Lab Notes

There is an option with static routes to specify an outbound local interface as next hop as well.

router-1(config)# **ip route 172.16.2.1 255.255.255.0 Fa1/0** <enter>
router-1(config)# **ip route 172.16.2.1 255.255.255.0 Fa1/0** <enter>

Lab 3-3: Default Route

Lab Summary: Configure a default route on router-1 for packet forwarding to all unknown destinations. The default route specifies the next hop address to forward packets when no route to the destination subnet exists in the routing table.

Figure 3-3 Lab Topology

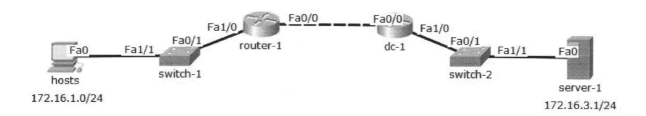

Lab Configuration

Start Packet Tracer File: **Lab 3-3 Default Route**

Step 1: Verify there is no current connectivity from host-1 to server-1: **c:\> ping 172.16.3.1** <enter>

Router-1

Click on the *router-1* icon and select the *CLI* folder. Hit the <enter> key for user mode prompt (>).

Step 2: Enter global configuration mode

    router-1> **enable** <enter>
    Password: **cisconet** <enter>
    router-1# **configure terminal** <enter>

Step 3: Configure a default route on router-1 with next hop of 192.168.1.2 (router-2 interface Fa0/0).

    router-1(config)# **ip route 0.0.0.0 0.0.0.0 192.168.1.2** <enter>
    router-1(config)# **end** <enter>
    router-1# **copy running-config startup-config** <enter>

DC-1

Click on the *dc-1* icon and select the *CLI* folder. Hit the <enter> key for user mode prompt (>).

Step 4: Enter global configuration mode

    dc-1> **enable** <enter>
    Password: **cisconet** <enter>
    dc-1# **configure terminal** <enter>

Step 5: Configure a static route on dc-1 for reachability to host-1 subnet (172.16.1.0/24)

dc-1(config)# **ip route 172.16.1.0 255.255.255.0 192.168.1.1** <enter>
dc-1(config)# **end** <enter>
dc-1# **copy running-config startup-config** <enter>

Step 6: <u>Verify Lab</u>

Verify the configuration is correct and confirm the default route with next hop 192.168.1.2 is installed in the routing table of router-1. In addition confirm there are no routes to 192.168.3.0 subnet in the routing table. Ping the data center server (192.168.3.1) to verify the default route is working correctly. Run the traceroute command as well to verify the route path from router-1 to server-1.

router-1# **show running-config** <enter>

router-1# **show ip route** <enter>

S*   0.0.0.0/0 [1/0] via 192.168.1.2 <enter>

dc-1# **show ip route** <enter>

S   172.16.1.0 [1/0] via 192.168.1.1 <enter>

host-1: **c:\> ping 172.16.3.1** <enter>

host-1: **c:\> tracert 172.16.3.1** <enter>

Lab 3-4: Subnetting (VLSM)

Lab Summary: Configure IP addressing for three new branch offices with the Class C addresses provided. In addition select subnet masks based on the maximum number of hosts required per segment.

Figure 3-4 Lab Topology

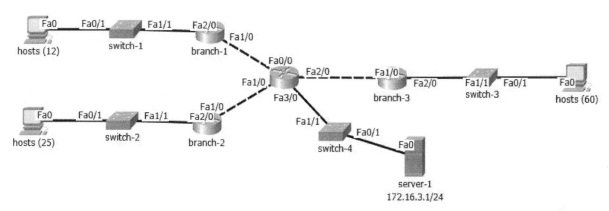

Lab Configuration

Start Packet Tracer File: **Lab 3-4 Subnetting**

Configure IP addressing for three new branch offices based on the following subnetting requirements.

Hostname	Hosts	LAN Segment	Subnet Mask	WAN Segment	Interface	Subnet Mask
Branch-1	12	192.168.10.1-14	255.255.255.240 (/28)	192.168.16.1	Fa1/0	255.255.255.252 (/30)
Branch-2	25	192.168.11.1-30	255.255.255.224 (/27)	192.168.16.5	Fa1/0	255.255.255.252 (/30)
Branch-3	60	192.168.12.1-62	255.255.255.192 (/26)	192.168.16.9	Fa1/0	255.255.255.252 (/30)
DC-1	2	-	-	192.168.16.2	Fa1/0	255.255.255.252 (/30)
DC-1	2	-	-	192.168.16.6	Fa1/0	255.255.255.252 (/30)
DC-1	2	-	-	192.168.16.10	Fa1/0	255.255.255.252 (/30)

Branch-1:

Click on *branch-1* router icon and select the *CLI* folder. Hit the <enter> key for user mode prompt (>).

Step 1: Enter global configuration mode

    branch-1> **enable** <enter>
    Password: **cisconet** <enter>
    branch-1# **configure terminal** <enter>

Step 2: Configure LAN interface Fa2/0

    branch-1(config)# **interface fastethernet2/0** <enter>
    branch-1(config-if)# **description LAN Interface** <enter>
    branch-1(config-if)# **ip address 192.168.10.14 255.255.255.240** <enter>
    branch-1(config-if)# **no shutdown** <enter>

Step 3: Configure WAN interface Fa1/0

    branch-1(config-if)# **interface fastethernet1/0** <enter>
    branch-1(config-if)# **description link to dc-1** <enter>
    branch-1(config-if)# **ip address 192.168.16.1 255.255.255.252** <enter>
    branch-1(config-if)# **no shutdown** <enter>
    branch-1(config)# **end** <enter>
    branch-1# **copy running-config startup-config** <enter>

Branch-2:

Click on *branch-2* router icon and select the *CLI* folder. Hit the <enter> key for user mode prompt (>).

Step 4: Enter global configuration mode

    branch-2> **enable** <enter>
    Password: **cisconet** <enter>
    branch-2# **configure terminal** <enter>

Step 5: Configure LAN interface Fa2/0

    branch-2(config)# **interface fastethernet2/0** <enter>
    branch-2(config-if)# **description LAN Interface** <enter>
    branch-2(config-if)# **ip address 192.168.11.30 255.255.255.224** <enter>
    branch-2(config-if)# **no shutdown** <enter>

Step 6: Configure WAN interface Fa1/0

    branch-2(config)# **interface fastethernet1/0** <enter>
    branch-2(config-if)# **description link to dc-1** <enter>
    branch-2(config-if)# **ip address 192.168.16.5 255.255.255.252** <enter>
    branch-2(config-if)# **no shutdown** <enter>
    branch-2(config)# **end** <enter>
    branch-2# **copy running-config startup-config** <enter>

Branch-3:

Click on *branch-3* router icon and select the *CLI* folder. Hit the <enter> key for user mode prompt (>).

Step 7: Enter global configuration mode

    branch-3> **enable** <enter>
    Password: **cisconet** <enter>
    branch-3# **configure terminal** <enter>

Step 8: Configure LAN interface Fa2/0

    branch-3(config)# **interface fastethernet2/0** <enter>
    branch-3(config-if)# **description LAN Interface** <enter>
    branch-3(config-if)# **ip address 192.168.12.62 255.255.255.192** <enter>
    branch-3(config-if)# **no shutdown** <enter>

Step 9: Configure WAN interface Fa1/0

    branch-3(config)# **interface fastethernet1/0** <enter>
    branch-3(config-if)# **description link to dc-1** <enter>
    branch-3(config-if)# **ip address 192.168.16.9 255.255.255.252** <enter>
    branch-3(config-if)# **no shutdown** <enter>

DC-1:

Click on *dc-1* router icon and select the *CLI* folder. Hit the <enter> key for user mode prompt (>).

Step 10: Enter global configuration mode

    dc-1> **enable** <enter>
    Password: **cisconet** <enter>
    dc-1# **configure terminal** <enter>

Step 11: Configure WAN interface Fa0/0

    dc-1(config)# **interface fastethernet0/0** <enter>
    dc-1(config-if)# **description link to branch-1** <enter>
    dc-1(config-if)# **ip address 192.168.16.2 255.255.255.252** <enter>
    dc-1(config-if)# **no shutdown** <enter>

Step 12: Configure WAN interface Fa1/0

    dc-1(config)# **interface fastethernet1/0** <enter>
    dc-1(config-if)# **description link to branch-2** <enter>
    dc-1(config-if)# **ip address 192.168.16.6 255.255.255.252** <enter>
    dc-1(config-if)# **no shutdown** <enter>

Step 13: Configure WAN interface Fa2/0

    dc-1(config)# **interface fastethernet2/0** <enter>
    dc-1(config-if)# **description link to branch-3** <enter>
    dc-1(config-if)# **ip address 192.168.16.10 255.255.255.252** <enter>
    dc-1(config-if)# **no shutdown** <enter>
    dc-1(config)# **end** <enter>
    dc-1# **copy running-config startup-config** <enter>

Step 14: Verify Lab

List the running configuration of each branch router to verify the IP address and subnet mask assigned are correct for LAN/WAN interfaces. In addition ping the neighbor interfaces and data center server from hosts at each branch.

branch-1# **show running-config** <enter>

branch-2# **show running-config** <enter>

branch-3# **show running-config** <enter>

hosts (branch-1)# **c:\> ping 172.16.3.1** <enter>

hosts (branch-2)# **c:\> ping 172.16.3.1** <enter>

hosts (branch-3)# **c:\> ping 172.16.3.1** <enter>

Lab Notes

The subnetting requirements are based on the number of new hosts considering there are often more network devices than employees. The following describes how the subnet mask length determines the maximum number of host assignments available. For instance with branch-1 the assigned subnet mask (/28) allocates 4 bits to the host portion. The binary conversion of $4^2 = 16$ hosts minus the network address (all zeros) and broadcast address (all ones). In addition there are 4 bits of the 4th octet are being subnetted from the Class C address. That allocates 16 subnets (4^2) with 14 host assignments per subnet. The subnets could be assigned to new branch offices for that region or new network devices.

The point-to-point WAN links require only two IP addresses and as a result typically are assigned the serial (/30) subnet mask. The loopback addresses are assigned as a host (/32) address and installed in the routing table with that prefix length.

Branch-1:
          network | hosts = 4 bits (1-14)
255.255.255.240 (/28) = **11111111.11111111.11111111.1111** 0000

Branch-2:
          network | hosts = 5 bits (1-30)
255.255.255.224 (/27) = **11111111.11111111.11111111.111** 00000

Branch-3:
          network | hosts = 6 bits (1-62)
255.255.255.192 (/26) = **11111111.11111111.11111111.11** 000000

Lab 3-5: Multi-Area OSPFv4

Lab Summary: Enable multi-area OSPF routing with a backbone area 0 and three stub areas for branch offices. Enable passive interfaces for filtering OSPF updates (LSA) to LAN switches.

Figure 3-5 Lab Topology

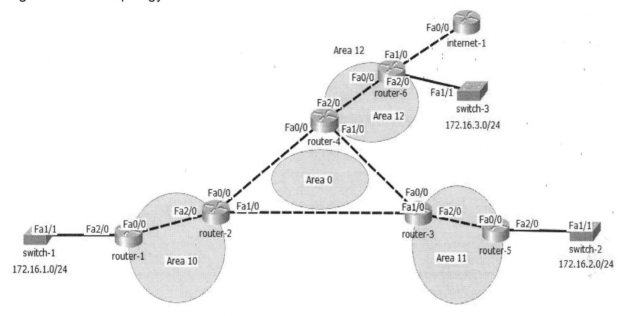

Lab Configuration

Start Packet Tracer File: **Lab 3-5 Multi-Area OSPFv4**

Router-2

Click on the *router-2* icon and select the *CLI* folder. Hit the <enter> key for user mode prompt (>).

Step 1: Enter global configuration mode

      router-2> **enable** <enter>
      Password: **cisconet** <enter>
      router-2# **configure terminal** <enter>

Step 2: Enable OSPF routing and assign process number 1 and router-id 192.168.255.1
      router-2(config)# **router ospf 1** <enter>
      router-2(config-router)# **router-id 192.168.255.1** <enter>

Step 3: Advertise the following subnets (prefixes) to OSPF neighbors and assign areas

      router-2(config-router)# **network 192.168.0.0 0.0.255.255 area 0** <enter>
      router-2(config-router)# **network 172.16.10.0 0.0.0.255 area 10** <enter>
      router-2(config-router)# **area 10 stub** <enter>
      router-2(config-router)# **end** <enter>
      router-2# **copy running-config startup-config** <enter>

Router-3

Click on the *router-3* icon and select the *CLI* folder. Hit the <enter> key for user mode prompt (>).

Step 4: Enter global configuration mode

 router-3> **enable** <enter>
 Password: **cisconet** <enter>
 router-3# **configure terminal** <enter>

Step 5: Enable OSPF routing and assign process number 1 and router-id 192.168.255.2

 router-3(config)# **router ospf 1** <enter>
 router-3(config-router)# **router-id 192.168.255.2** <enter>

Step 6: Advertise the following subnets (prefixes) to OSPF neighbors and assign areas

 router-3(config-router)# **network 192.168.0.0 0.0.255.255 area 0** <enter>
 router-3(config-router)# **network 172.16.11.0 0.0.0.255 area 11** <enter>
 router-3(config-router)# **area 11 stub** <enter>
 router-3(config-router)# **end** <enter>
 router-3# **copy running-config startup-config** <enter>

Router-4

Click on the *router-4* icon and select the *CLI* folder. Hit the <enter> key for user mode prompt (>).

Step 7: Enter global configuration mode

 router-4> **enable** <enter>
 Password: **cisconet** <enter>
 router-4# **configure terminal** <enter>

Step 8: Enable OSPF routing and assign process number 1 and router-id 192.168.255.3

 router-4(config)# **router ospf 1** <enter>
 router-4(config-router)# **router-id 192.168.255.3** <enter>

Step 9: Advertise the following subnets (prefixes) to OSPF neighbors and assign areas

 router-4(config-router)# **network 192.168.0.0 0.0.255.255 area 0** <enter>
 router-4(config-router)# **network 172.16.12.0 0.0.0.255 area 12** <enter>
 router-4(config-router)# **area 12 stub** <enter>
 router-4(config-router)# **end** <enter>
 router-4# **copy running-config startup-config** <enter>

Router-1

Click on the *router-1* icon and select the *CLI* folder. Hit the <enter> key for user mode prompt (>).

Step 10: Enter global configuration mode

> router-1> **enable** <enter>
> Password: **cisconet** <enter>
> router-1# **configure terminal** <enter>

Step 11: Enable OSPF routing and assign process number 1 and router-id 172.16.255.1

> router-1(config)# **router ospf 1** <enter>
> router-1(config-router)# **router-id 172.16.255.1** <enter>

Step 12: Advertise the following subnet (prefix) to OSPF neighbor and assign area 10

> router-1(config-router)# **network 172.16.10.0 0.0.0.255 area 10** <enter>
> router-1(config-router)# **network 172.16.1.0 0.0.0.255 area 10** <enter>
> router-1(config-router)# **area 10 stub** <enter>

Step 13: Configure interface Fa2/0 as OSPF passive

> router-1(config-router)# **passive-interface fastethernet2/0** <enter>
> router-1(config-router)# **end** <enter>
> router-1# **copy running-config startup-config** <enter>

Router-5

Click on the *router-5* icon and select the *CLI* folder. Hit the <enter> key for user mode prompt (>).

Step 14: Enter global configuration mode

> router-5> **enable** <enter>
> Password: **cisconet** <enter>
> router-5# **configure terminal** <enter>

Step 15: Enable OSPF routing and assign process number 1 and router-id 172.16.255.2

> router-5(config)# **router ospf 1** <enter>
> router-5(config-router)# **router-id 172.16.255.2** <enter>

Step 16: Advertise the following subnet (prefix) to OSPF neighbor and assign area 11

> router-5(config-router)# **network 172.16.11.0 0.0.0.255 area 11** <enter>
> router-5(config-router)# **network 172.16.2.0 0.0.0.255 area 11** <enter>
> router-5(config-router)# **area 11 stub** <enter>

Step 17: Configure interface Fa2/0 as OSPF passive

    router-5(config-router)# **passive-interface fastethernet2/0** <enter>
    router-5(config-router)# **end** <enter>
    router-5# **copy running-config startup-config** <enter>

Router-6

Click on the *router-6* icon and select the *CLI* folder. Hit the <enter> key for user mode prompt (>).

Step 18: Enter global configuration mode

    router-6> **enable** <enter>
    Password: **cisconet** <enter>
    router-6# **configure terminal** <enter>

Step 19: Enable OSPF routing and assign process number 1 and router-id 172.16.255.3

    router-6(config)# **router ospf 1** <enter>
    router-6(config-router)# **router-id 172.16.255.3** <enter>

Step 20: Advertise the following subnet (prefix) to OSPF neighbor and assign area 12

    router-6(config-router)# **network 172.16.12.0 0.0.0.255 area 12** <enter>
    router-6(config-router)# **network 172.16.3.0 0.0.0.255 area 12** <enter>
    router-6(config-router)# **area 12 stub** <enter>

Step 21: Configure interface Fa2/0 as OSPF passive

    router-6(config-router)# **passive-interface fastethernet2/0** <enter>
    router-6(config-router)# **end** <enter>
    router-6# **copy running-config startup-config** <enter>

Step 22: <u>Verify Lab:</u>

Verify the configuration is correct on all routers and confirm OSPF neighbor adjacencies based on the router-id. Verify interface Fa2/0 on router-1, router-5 and router-6 are passive with **show ip ospf interface** command. Verify all connected subnets and neighbor routes are installed in the local routing table. Ping between all directly connected interfaces to verify layer 3 connectivity. Ping from router-1 to all LAN segments to verify routing is working correctly across the network.

    router# **show running-config** <enter>

    router-2# **show ip ospf neighbor** <enter>

Neighbor ID	Pri	State	Dead Time	Address	Interface
172.16.255.1	1	2WAY/DROTHER	00:00:36	172.16.10.1	FastEthernet2/0
192.168.255.3	1	2WAY/DROTHER	00:00:36	192.168.2.2	FastEthernet0/0
192.168.255.2	1	2WAY/DROTHER	00:00:36	192.168.1.2	FastEthernet1/0

    router-3# **show ip ospf neighbor** <enter>

    router-4# **show ip ospf neighbor** <enter>

router-1# **show ip ospf interface fastethernet2/0** <enter>

router-2# **show ip route** <enter>

router-1# **ping** [*neighbor interfaces*] <enter>

router-1# **ping 172.16.2.1** <enter>

router-1# **ping 172.16.3.1** <enter>

router-1# **ping 172.33.1.2** <enter>

Lab Notes

OSPF **network area** commands enable OSPF routing on local interfaces that are within the subnet range specified. This lab advertises all connected subnets to OSPF neighbors. The route advertised is for an interface address that provides the most specific route. The routes are advertised only to the area specified as well.

OSPF is a classless routing protocol where wildcard masks are required to define subnets for advertising. OSPF passive interfaces are typically configured on LAN interfaces of routers where OSPF is enabled. The LAN subnet 172.16.1.0 for instance is advertised from interface Fa2/0 as an OSPF route to area 10. The interface is configured as passive allowing OSPF routing updates however they do not forward them to the switch. That is often configured when there is a link to another routing domain as well. There are security issues that can result from sending OSPF routing updates where there are no OSPF neighbors.

Lab 3-6: EIGRP for IPv4

Lab Summary: Configure EIGRPv4 on all routers, advertise all connected subnets and turn off automatic route summarization.

Figure 3-6 Lab Topology

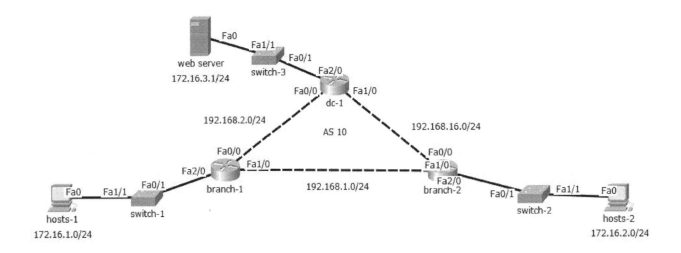

Lab Configuration

Start Packet Tracer File: **Lab 3-6 EIGRP for IPv4**

Branch-1

Click on the *Branch-1* icon and select the *CLI* folder. Hit the <enter> key for user mode prompt (>).

Step 1: Enter global configuration mode

     branch-1> **enable** <enter>
     Password: **cisconet** <enter>
     branch-1# **configure terminal** <enter>

Step 2: Enable EIGRP and assign to AS 10

     branch-1(config)# **router eigrp 10** <enter>

Step 3: Advertise the following subnets (prefixes) to EIGRP neighbors

     branch-1(config-router)# **network 192.168.1.0 0.0.0.255** <enter>
     branch-1(config-router)# **network 192.168.2.0 0.0.0.255** <enter>
     branch-1(config-router)# **network 172.16.1.0 0.0.0.255** <enter>

Step 4: Turn off automatic summarization of routes on default class boundaries

      branch-1(config-router)# **no auto-summary** <enter>
      branch-1(config-router)# **end** <enter>
      branch-1# **copy running-config startup-config** <enter>

Branch-2

Click on the *branch-2* icon and select the *CLI* folder. Hit the <enter> key for user mode prompt (>).

Step 5: Enter global configuration mode

      branch-2> **enable** <enter>
      Password: **cisconet** <enter>
      branch-2# **configure terminal** <enter>

Step 6: Enable EIGRP and assign to AS 10

      branch-2(config)# **router eigrp 10** <enter>

Step 7: Advertise the following subnets (prefixes) to EIGRP neighbors

      branch-2(config-router)# **network 192.168.2.0 0.0.0.255** <enter>
      branch-2(config-router)# **network 192.168.16.0 0.0.0.255** <enter>
      branch-2(config-router)# **network 172.16.2.0 0.0.0.255** <enter>

Step 8: Turn off automatic summarization of routes on default class boundaries

      branch-2(config-router)# **no auto-summary** <enter>
      branch-2(config-router)# **end** <enter>
      branch-2# **copy running-config startup-config** <enter>

DC-1

Click on the *dc-1* icon and select the *CLI* folder. Hit the <enter> key for user mode prompt (>).

Step 9: Enter global configuration mode

      dc-1> **enable** <enter>
      Password: **cisconet** <enter>
      dc-1# **configure terminal** <enter>

Step 10: Enable EIGRP and assign to AS 10

      dc-1(config)# **router eigrp 10** <enter>

Step 11: Advertise the following subnets (prefixes) to EIGRP neighbor

      dc-1(config-router)# **network 192.168.2.0 0.0.0.255** <enter>
      dc-1(config-router)# **network 192.168.16.0 0.0.0.255** <enter>
      dc-1(config-router)# **network 172.16.3.0 0.0.0.255** <enter>

Step 12: Turn off automatic summarization of routes on default class boundaries

>dc-1(config-router)# **no auto-summary** <enter>
>dc-1(config-router)# **end** <enter>
>dc-1# **copy running-config startup-config** <enter>

Step 13: Verify Lab:

Verify the configuration is correct and confirm EIGRP adjacency between all routers. Confirm branch-1 has interfaces Fa0/0 and Fa1/0 assigned to AS 10. Verify connected and neighbor advertised subnets are installed in the routing table of each router. Ping between all router connected interfaces to verify layer 3 connectivity. Ping server-1 from hosts-1 and hosts-2 to verify routing is working correctly.

>branch-1# **show running-config** <enter>

>branch-1# **show ip eigrp neighbors** <enter>

IP-EIGRP neighbors for process 10

H	Address	Interface	Hold Uptime (sec)	SRTT (ms)	RTO	Q Cnt	Seq Num
0	192.168.2.2	Fa0/0	14 00:00:46	40	1000	0	7
1	192.168.1.2	Fa1/0	11 00:00:46	40	1000	0	7

>branch-2# **show ip eigrp neighbors** <enter>

>branch-1# **show ip route** <enter>

172.16.0.0/24 is subnetted, 3 subnets
C   172.16.1.0 is directly connected, FastEthernet2/0
D   172.16.2.0 [90/30720] via 192.168.1.2, 00:00:16, FastEthernet1/0
D   172.16.3.0 [90/30720] via 192.168.2.2, 00:00:16, FastEthernet0/0
C 192.168.1.0/24 is directly connected, FastEthernet1/0
C 192.168.2.0/24 is directly connected, FastEthernet0/0
D 192.168.16.0/24 [90/30720] via 192.168.1.2, 00:00:16, FastEthernet1/0
    [90/30720] via 192.168.2.2, 00:00:16, FastEthernet0/0

>branch-1# **ping** [*neighbor interface*] <enter>

>hosts-1: **c:\> ping 172.16.3.1** <enter>

>hosts-2: **c:\> ping 172.16.3.1** <enter>

Lab Notes

The **network** command would advertise all subnets from all interfaces within the specified subnet range. There is support for classless routing with wildcard masks and **no auto-summary** command. For instance **network 172.16.1.0 0.0.0.255** command advertises 172.16.1.0/24 subnet (route) to EIGRP neighbors from the local interface assigned within that same subnet.

There is no wildcard mask required when advertising EIGRP classful subnets. For instance **network 172.16.0.0** command would advertise all 172.16.0.0/16 subnets to EIGRP neighbors. The routes would be advertised from all local interfaces assigned within that same subnet range. EIGRP enabled routers can only advertises routes within the same autonomous system (AS) as well. As a result the AS number assigned to each router must match to form neighbor adjacencies.

Lab 3-7: RIPv2

Lab Summary: Enable RIPv2 on all routers and advertise all connected subnets to neighbors. In addition turn off automatic summarization and advertise a default route from dc-1 to all neighbors.

Figure 3-7 Lab Topology

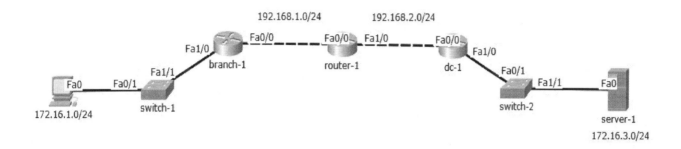

Lab Configuration

Start Packet Tracer File: **Lab 3-7 RIPv2**

Branch-1

Click on the *branch-1* icon and select the *CLI* folder. Hit the <enter> key for user mode prompt (>).

Step 1: Enter global configuration mode

    branch-1> **enable** <enter>
    Password: **cisconet** <enter>
    branch-1# **configure terminal** <enter>

Step 2: Enable RIPv2 on branch-1 router

    branch-1(config)# **router rip** <enter>
    branch-1(config-router)# **version 2** <enter>

Step 3: Enable advertising of all connected subnets to RIPv2 neighbors

    branch-1(config-router)# **network 192.168.1.0** <enter>
    branch-1(config-router)# **network 172.16.0.0** <enter>

Step 4: Turn off automatic summarization to advertise classless routes

    branch-1(config-router)# **no auto-summary** <enter>
    branch-1(config-router)# **end** <enter>
    branch-1# **copy running-config startup-config** <enter>

Router-1

Click on the *router-1* icon and select the *CLI* folder. Hit the <enter> key for user mode prompt (>).

Step 5: Enter global configuration mode

    router-1> **enable** <enter>
    Password: **cisconet** <enter>
    router-1# **configure terminal** <enter>

Step 6: Enable RIPv2 on router-2

    router-1(config)# **router rip** <enter>
    router-1(config-router)# **version 2** <enter>

Step 7: Enable advertising of all connected subnets to RIPv2 neighbors

    router-1(config-router)# **network 192.168.1.0** <enter>
    router-1(config-router)# **network 192.168.2.0** <enter>

Step 8: Turn off automatic summarization to advertise classless routes

    router-1(config-router)# **no auto-summary** <enter>
    router-1(config-router)# **end** <enter>
    router-1# **copy running-config startup-config** <enter>

DC-1

Click on the *dc-1* icon and select the *CLI* folder. Hit the <enter> key for user mode prompt (>).

Step 9: Enter global configuration mode

    dc-1> **enable** <enter>
    Password: **cisconet** <enter>
    dc-1# **configure terminal** <enter>

Step 10: Enable RIPv2 on dc-1

    dc-1(config)# **router rip** <enter>
    dc-1(config-router)# **version 2** <enter>

Step 11: Enable advertising of all connected subnets to RIPv2 neighbor

    dc-1(config-router)# **network 192.168.2.0** <enter>
    dc-1(config-router)# **network 172.16.0.0** <enter>

Step 12: Turn off automatic summarization to advertise classless routes

    dc-1(config-router)# **no auto-summary** <enter>

Step 13: Advertise a default route to all RIPv2 neighbors for any unknown routes

dc-1(config-router)# **default-information originate** <enter>
dc-1(config-router)# **end** <enter>
dc-1# **copy running-config startup-config** <enter>

Step 14: <u>Verify Lab</u>

Verify the configuration is correct and confirm that connected subnets and routes advertised from neighbors are installed in the local routing table. In addition confirm and ping between all router connected interfaces and server-1 to verify layer 3 connectivity. Run traceroute to server-1 and verify the routing path is correct. Run traceroute to any route not in the routing table and verify packets are dropped at dc-1 router. That confirms RIPv2 is advertising the default route to router- and router-2. The packet is dropped at dc-1 since there is no internet connectivity (or route to the destination subnet).

branch-1# **show running-config** <enter>

branch-1# **show ip route** <enter>

branch-1# **ping** [*neighbor interface*] <enter>

host: **c:\> ping 172.16.3.1** <enter>

host: **c:\> tracert 172.16.3.1** <enter>

host: **c:\> tracert 172.33.1.1** <enter>

<u>Lab Notes</u>

The **network** command for RIPv2 as with OSPF and EIGRP specify subnets (routes) to advertise from local interfaces assigned within the same range. The **network** statement however only supports classful subnets with no subnet mask or wildcard mask. For instance RIPv2 would change the **network 172.16.1.0** command to **network 172.16.0.0**. The **no auto-summary** command enables classless routing where the subnet mask is included with routing advertisements. RIPv2 would then advertise 172.16.1.0 to neighbors from the local interface assigned to that subnet.

Lab 3-8: Named ACL

Lab Summary:

Configure a named access control list (ACL) to filter traffic based on the following requirements:

1. Configure a named ACL called *http-telnet-filter*
2. Add a remark that describes the purpose of the ACL
3. Permit all HTTP traffic from hosts on 192.168.0.0/24 subnets to the web server
4. Deny Telnet sessions from hosts on 192.168.0.0/24 subnets to all routers
5. Permit all traffic not matching on any previous ACL statements
6. Apply the named ACL *http-telnet filter* inbound on router-1 interface Fa2/0

Figure 3-8 Lab Topology

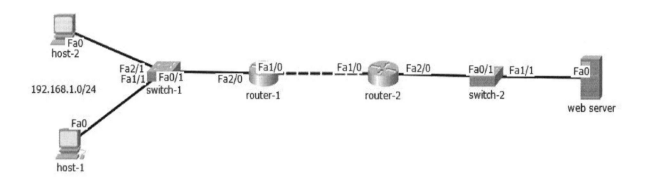

Lab Configuration

Start Packet Tracer File: **Lab 3-8 Named ACL**

Verify that currently there is web server and telnet access permitted from host-1 and host-2:

> host-1: **http://192.168.3.1** <enter> **(yes)**
> host-1# **c:\> telnet 192.168.2.1** <enter> **(yes)** password: *cisco*
> host-1# **c:\> telnet 192.168.2.2** <enter> **(yes)** password: *cisco*
> host-2: **http://192.168.3.1** <enter> **(yes)**
> host-2# **c:\> telnet 192.168.2.1** <enter> **(yes)** password: *cisco*
> host-2# **c:\> telnet 192.168.2.2** <enter> **(yes)** password: *cisco*

Click on the *router-1* icon and select the *CLI* folder. Hit the <enter> key for user mode prompt (>).

Step 1: Enter global configuration mode

> router-1> **enable** <enter>
> Password: **cisconet** <enter>
> router-1# **configure terminal** <enter>

Step 2: Create a named ACL called *http-telnet-filter* and add a remark to explain its purpose

    router-1(config)# **ip access-list extended http-telnet-filter** <enter>
    router-1(config-ext-nacl)# **remark deny access to web server and telnet sessions** <enter>

Step 3: Permit HTTP from hosts on 192.168.0.0/24 subnets to the web server

    router-1(config-ext-nacl)# **deny tcp 192.168.0.0 0.0.255.255 host 192.168.3.1 eq www** <enter>

Step 4: Deny Telnet sessions from hosts on 192.168.0.0/24 subnets to any router

    router-1(config-ext-nacl)# **deny tcp 192.168.0.0 0.0.255.255 any eq telnet** <enter>

Step 5: Permit all traffic from hosts that does not match any previous ACL statements

    router-1(config-ext-nacl)# **permit ip any any** <enter>
    router-1(config-ext-nacl)# **exit** <enter>

Step 6: Apply the named ACL inbound on router-1 interface Fa2/0 and save the running configuration.

    router-1(config)# **interface fastethernet2/0** <enter>
    router-1(config-if)# **ip access-group http-telnet-filter in** <enter>
    router-1(config-if)# **end** <enter>
    router-1# **copy running-config startup-config** <enter>

Step 7: <u>Verify Lab</u>

Verify the ACL configuration is correct and confirm that it is enabled. Start the web browser from host-1 and host-2 to verify access to the web server is permitted. In addition confirm there is no Telnet access permitted from hosts to any router. There is however Telnet access available from the routers. The ACL is applied inbound on router-1 and does not filter past that point.

    router-1# **show running-config** <enter>

    router-1# **show access-lists** <enter>

    Extended IP access list http-telnet-filter
        10 deny tcp 192.168.0.0 0.0.255.255 host 192.168.3.1 eq www
        20 deny tcp 192.168.0.0 0.0.255.255 any eq telnet
        30 permit ip any any

    host-1: **http://192.168.3.1** <enter> **(no)**

    host-1# **c:\> telnet 192.168.2.1** <enter> **(no)**

    host-1# **c:\> telnet 192.168.2.2** <enter> **(no)**

    host-2: **http://192.168.3.1** <enter> **(no)**

    host-2# **c:\> telnet 192.168.2.1** <enter> **(no)**

    host-2# **c:\> telnet 192.168.2.2** <enter> **(no)**

    router-1# **telnet 192.168.2.2** <enter> **(yes)**

Remove the ACL from router-1 interface FastEthernet2/0 and verify access is now available.

     router-1(config)# **no ip access-group http-telnet-filter in**

<u>Lab Notes:</u>

The **show access-lists** command is available for troubleshooting packet filtering that includes each statement per ACL and the specific order. The access control list (ACL) statements are numbered starting with 10 and verify how packet matching is occurring. Note as well that deleting a statement and adding a new statement will assign the ACL to the bottom of the list. That could then affect how packet matching is occurring and inadvertently permit/deny wrong traffic.

Lab 3-9: Extended Access Control List (ACL)

Lab Summary:

Configure an extended access control list (ACL) to filter traffic based on the following requirements:

1. Configure extended access list number 100
2. Add a remark that describes the purpose of the ACL
3. Deny all FTP traffic from hosts on subnet 192.168.1.0/24 to the FTP server
4. Deny HTTP traffic only from host-2 to the web server
5. Permit all traffic not matching on any previous ACL statements
6. Apply ACL 100 inbound on R1 interface Fa2/0

Figure 3-9 Lab Topology

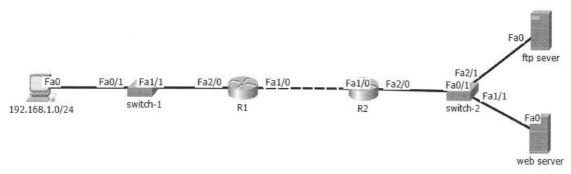

Lab Configuration

Start Packet Tracer File: **Lab 3-9 Extended ACL**

Verify that currently there is ftp server and web server access permitted from host-1 and host-2:

    host-1: **c:\> ftp 192.168.3.1** <enter> username *cisco* / password *cisco* **(yes)**
    host-1: **http://192.168.3.2** <enter> **(yes)**
    host-2: **c:\> ftp 192.168.3.1** <enter> username *cisco* / password *cisco* **(yes)**
    host-2: **http://192.168.3.2** <enter> **(yes)**

Click on the *R1* icon and select the *CLI* folder. Hit the <enter> key for user mode prompt (>).

Step 1: Enter global configuration mode

    R1> **enable** <enter>
    Password: **cisconet** <enter>
    R1# **configure terminal** <enter>

Step 2: Deny FTP traffic from hosts on subnet 192.168.1.0/24 to the FTP server

 R1(config-ext-acl)# **access-list 100 deny tcp 192.168.1.0 0.0.0.255 host 192.168.3.1 eq ftp** <enter>

Step 3: Deny HTTP traffic only from 192.168.1.2/24 (host-2) to the web server.

R1(config-ext-acl)# **access-list 100 deny tcp host 192.168.1.2 host 192.168.3.2 eq www** <enter>

Step 4: Permit all traffic that does not match any previous ACL 100 statements

R1(config-ext-acl)# **access-list 100 permit ip any any** <enter>
R1(config-ext-acl)# **exit** <enter>

Step 5: Apply ACL 100 inbound on R1 interface Fa2/0 and save the running configuration.

    R1(config)# **interface fastethernet2/0** <enter>
    R1(config-if)# **ip access-group 100 in** <enter>
    R1(config-if)# **end** <enter>
    R1# **copy running-config startup-config** <enter>

Step 6: <u>Verify Lab</u>

Verify ACL 100 configuration is correct and confirm ip access group 100 is applied to router-1 interface FastEthermet2/0. Confirm access to FTP server (192.168.3.2) is denied from host-1 and host-2. In addition confirm host-1 is permitted and host-2 is denied access to the web server (192.168.3.2).

    R1# **show running-config** <enter>

    R1# **show access-lists** <enter>

    Extended IP access list 100
        10 deny tcp 192.168.1.0 0.0.0.255 host 192.168.3.1 eq ftp
        20 deny tcp host 192.168.1.2 host 192.168.3.2 eq www
        30 permit ip any any

host-1: **c:\> ftp 192.168.3.1** <enter> **(no)**

host-1: **http://192.168.3.2** <enter> **(yes)**

host-2: **c:\> ftp 192.168.3.1** <enter> **(no)**

host-2: **http://192.168.3.2** <enter> **(no)**

Lab 3-10: Port Address Translation (NAT Overload)

Lab Summary: Configure port address translation based on a pool of assigned public IP addresses from the ISP. In addition permit all internal hosts assigned to 192.168.0.0/24 subnets access to the internet.

Figure 3-10 Lab Topology

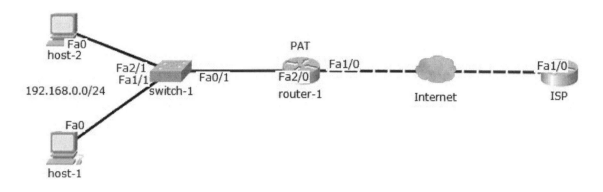

Lab Configuration

Start Packet Tracer File: **Lab 3-10 Port Address Translation**

Click on the *Router-1* icon and select the *CLI* folder. Hit the <enter> key for user mode prompt (>).

Step 1: Enter global configuration mode

    router-1 > **enable** <enter>
    Password: **cisconet** <enter>
    router-1# **configure terminal** <enter>

Step 2: Assign the inside NAT interface on router-1

    router-1(config)# **interface fastethernet2/0** <enter>
    router-1(config)# **ip address 192.168.1.3 255.255.255.0** <enter>
    router-1(config-if)# **ip nat inside** <enter>
    router-1(config-if)# **no shutdown** <enter>
    router-1(config-if)# **exit** <enter>

Step 3: Assign the outside NAT interface on router-1

    router-1(config)# **interface fastethernet1/0** <enter>
    router-1(config-if)# **ip address 172.33.1.1 255.255.255.0** <enter>
    router-1(config-if)# **ip nat outside** <enter>
    router-1(config-if)# **no shutdown** <enter>
    router-1(config-if)# **exit** <enter>

Step 4: Create pool name *cisconet* and assign public IP address range 172.33.1.1 - 172.33.1.10

    router-1(config)# **ip nat pool cisconet 172.33.1.1 172.33.1.10 netmask 255.255.255.0** <enter>

Step 5: Configure ACL 100 to permit host IP address range 192.168.0.0 - 192.168.255.255

    router-1(config)# **access-list 100 permit ip 192.168.0.0 0.0.255.255 any** <enter>

Step 6: Assign ACL 100 to pool name *cisconet* and enable port address translation

    router-1(config)# **ip nat inside source list 100 pool cisconet overload** <enter>
    router-1(config)# **end** <enter>
    router-1# **copy running-config startup-config** <enter>

Step 7: Verify Lab

Confirm the configuration is correct and ping the internet web server to verify port address translation is working correctly. The translation table lists the inside host IP address (192.168.1.1) and public IP address allocated from pool *cisconet* (172.33.1.1-10).

    router-1# **show running-config** <enter>

    host-1: **c:\> ping 172.33.1.254** <enter>

    router-1# **show ip nat translations** <enter>

Pro	Inside global	Inside local	Outside local	Outside global
icmp	172.33.1.1:2	192.168.1.1:2	172.33.1.2:2	172.33.1.2:2
icmp	172.33.1.1:3	192.168.1.1:3	172.33.1.254:3	172.33.1.254:3
icmp	172.33.1.1:4	192.168.1.1:4	172.33.1.254:4	172.33.1.254:4
icmp	172.33.1.1:5	192.168.1.1:5	172.33.1.254:5	172.33.1.254:5
icmp	172.33.1.1:6	192.168.1.1:6	172.33.1.254:6	172.33.1.254:6

Lab 3-11: Router Management

Lab Summary: Configure loopback interfaces on router-1, router-2 and router-3 for management
        purposes. In addition configure a loopback interface on the internet-1 router and enable
        SSH (encrypted) remote access.

Figure 3-11 Lab Topology

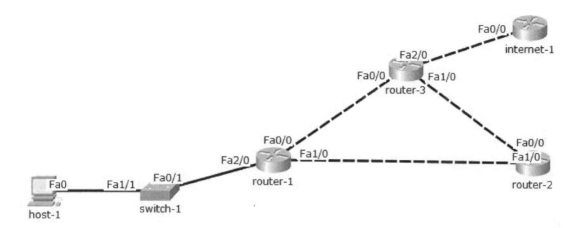

Lab Configuration:

Start Packet Tracer File: **Lab 3-11 Router Management**

Router-1

Click on the *router-1* icon and select the *CLI* folder. Hit the <enter> key for user mode prompt (>).

Step 1: Enter global configuration mode

>   router-1 > **enable** <enter>
>   router-1# **configure terminal** <enter>

Step 2: Configure enable password *cisconet*

>   router-1(config)# **enable password cisconet** <enter>

Step 3: Configure a management loopback0 interface 192.168.255.1/32

>   router-1(config)# **interface Loopback 0** <enter>
>   router-1(config-if)# **description management interface** <enter>
>   router-1(config-if)# **ip address 192.168.255.1 255.255.255.255** <enter>
>   router-1(config-if)# **no shutdown** <enter>
>   router-1(config-if)# **exit** <enter>

Step 4: Configure VTY lines 0 4 for Telnet login access with password *ccnalabs and* save the running configuration.

```
router-1(config)# line vty 0 4 <enter>
router-1(config-line)# password ccnalabs <enter>
router-1(config-line)# login <enter>
router-1(config-line)# end <enter>
router-1# copy running-config startup-config <enter>
```

Router-2

Click on the *router-2* icon and select the *CLI* folder. Hit the <enter> key for user mode prompt (>).

Step 5: Enter global configuration mode

```
router-2 > enable <enter>
router-2# configure terminal <enter>
```

Step 6: Configure enable password *cisconet*

```
router-2(config)# enable password cisconet
```

Step 7: Configure a management loopback0 interface 192.168.255.2/32

```
router-2(config)# interface Loopback 0 <enter>
router-2(config-if)# description management interface <enter>
router-2(config-if)# ip address 192.168.255.2 255.255.255.255 <enter>
router-2(config-if)# no shutdown <enter>
router-2(config-if)# exit <enter>
```

Step 8: Configure username cisco with password ccnalabs (local authentication)

```
router-2(config)# username cisco password ccnalabs <enter>
```

Step 9: Configure VTY lines 0 4 for Telnet access with password *ccnalabs*.

```
router-2(config)# line vty 0 4 <enter>
router-2(config-line)# login local <enter>
router-2(config-line)# end <enter>
router-2# copy running-config startup-config <enter>
```

Router-3

Click on the *router-3* icon and select the *CLI* folder. Hit the <enter> key for user mode prompt (>).

Step 10: Enter global configuration mode

```
router-3 > enable <enter>
router-3# configure terminal <enter>
```

Step 11: Configure a management loopback0 interface 192.168.255.3/32

    router-3(config)# **interface Loopback 0** <enter>
    router-3(config-if)# **description management interface** <enter>
    router-3(config-if)# **ip address 192.168.255.3 255.255.255.255** <enter>
    router-3(config-if)# **no shutdown** <enter>
    router-3(config-if)# **exit** <enter>

Step 12: Configure username cisco with privilege level 15 and password ccnalabs (local authentication)

    router-3(config)# **username cisco privilege 15 password ccnalabs** <enter>

Step 13: Configure VTY lines 0 4 for Telnet local authentication and save the running configuration.

    router-3(config)# **line vty 0 4** <enter>
    router-3(config-line)# **login local** <enter>
    router-3(config-line)# **end** <enter>
    router-3# **copy running-config startup-config** <enter>

Internet-1

Click on the *internet-1* icon and select the *CLI* folder. Hit the <enter> key for user mode prompt (>).

Step 14: Enter global configuration mode

    internet-1 > **enable** <enter>
    internet-1# **configure terminal** <enter>

Step 15: Configure a management loopback0 interface 192.168.255.4/32

    internet-1(config)# **interface Loopback 0** <enter>
    internet-1(config-if)# **description management interface** <enter>
    internet-1(config-if)# **ip address 192.168.255.4 255.255.255.255** <enter>
    internet-1(config-if)# **no shutdown** <enter>
    internet-1(config-if)# **exit** <enter>

Step 16: Enable SSH (encrypted) access to the internet router.

    internet-1(config)# **ip domain-name lab.cisconet.com** <enter>
    internet-1(config)# **username admin privilege 15 password ccnalabs** <enter>
    internet-1(config)# **crypto key generate rsa** <enter>
        [type *yes* to create key]
        bits? [*768*] <enter>
    internet-1(config)# **ip ssh version 2** <enter>
    internet-1(config)# **ip ssh time-out 60** <enter>

Step 17: Allow SSH access only with local login authentication to the internet router.

    internet-1#(config)# **line vty 0 4** <enter>
    internet-1#(config)# **login local** <enter>
    internet-1#(config-line)# **transport input ssh** <enter>
    internet-1(config-line)# **end** <enter>
    internet-1# **copy running-config startup-config** <enter>

Step 18: Verify Lab

Confirm the configuration is correct and the loopback interfaces are operational on all routers. Start a Telnet session to router-1, router-2 and router-2 and confirm it is working. Make note of the passwords required for each router. Attempt to access internet-1 with Telnet verifying it is denied to that router. In addition confirm SSH login to the internet router is working correctly.

    router-1# **show running-config** <enter>

    internet-1# **show running-config** <enter>

    router-1# **ping 192.168.255.2** <enter>

    router-1# **ping 192.168.255.3** <enter>

    router-1# **ping 192.168.255.4** <enter>

    internet-1# **ping 192.168.255.1** <enter>

    router-1# **show interfaces loopback0** <enter>

Telnet to each router from host-1 (or neighbor router)

    host-1: **c:\> telnet 192.168.255.1** <enter>
    VTY password: **ccnalabs** <enter>
    enable password: **cisconet** <enter>

    host-1: **c:\> telnet 192.168.255.2** <enter>
    username: **cisco** <enter>
    VTY Password: **ccnalabs** <enter>
    enable password: **cisconet** <enter>

    host-1: **c:\> telnet 192.168.255.3** <enter>
    username: **cisco** <enter>
    password: **ccnalabs** <enter>

SSH to internet-1 from host-1 (or any neighbor router)

    host-1: **c:\> ssh –l admin 192.168.255.4** <enter>
    password: **ccnalabs** <enter>

Telnet to switch-1 from router-3 (optional)

    internet-1# **telnet 172.16.1.2** <enter>
    VTY password: **ccnalabs** <enter>
    enable password: **cisconet** <enter>

Lab Notes

The enable password is only required on router-1 and router-2 where there is no privilege level 15 configured. There is access to switch-1 with the management SVI, default gateway and VTY line enabled. Telnet initiates the session to the switch-1 management SVI address (172.16.1.2/24).

Lab 3-12: Password Recovery

Lab Summary: Perform password recovery on a router where a new password was configured by a contractor and unknown to technical support staff.

Figure 3-12 Lab Topology

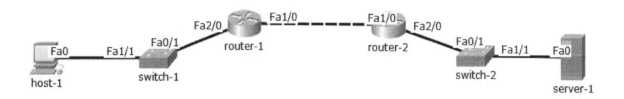

Lab Configuration

Start Packet Tracer File: **Lab 3-12 Password Recovery**

Click on the *router-1* icon and select the *CLI* folder. Hit the <enter> key for user mode prompt (>).

Step 1: Enter global configuration mode

    router-1 > **enable** <enter>
    Password: **cisconet** <enter> <enter> <enter>
    router-1# **configure terminal** <enter>

Step 2: Select *Physical* folder and use right arrow key to shift right and toggle power switch off/on to restart router-1. Now go quickly to step 3.

Step 3: Select *CLI* folder and press *<Ctrl>* + *<C>* keys to start ROMmon mode

Step 4: Modify the configuration register to prevent the startup configuration file from loading:

    rommon 1 > **confreg 0x2142** <enter>

Step 5: Reboot router-1 with the following IOS command from ROMmon mode:

    rommon 2 > **reset** <enter>

Step 6: Issue the following IOS command to load the startup configuration to NVRAM :

    Continue with configuration dialog? [yes/no] **no** <enter> <enter>
    router-1 > **enable** <enter>
    router-1# **copy startup-config running-config** <enter> <enter>

Step 7: Change the password to *cisconet* and save changes with the following IOS commands:

    router-1# **configure terminal** <enter>
    router-1(config)# **enable password cisconet** <enter>
    router-1(config)# **exit** <enter> <enter>
    router-1# **copy running-config startup-config** <enter> <enter>

Step 8: Modify the configuration register with the following IOS command and restart router-1:

     router-1# **configure terminal** <enter>
     router-1(config)# **config-register 0x2102** <enter>
     router-1(config)# **end** <enter> <enter>
     router-1# **reload** <enter> <enter>

Step 9: Sign-on with the new password to verify

     router-1 > **enable** <enter>
     Password: **cisconet** <enter>

If this does not work call the contractor (some humour !)

Lab 3-13: Inter-VLAN Routing

Lab Summary: Configure three switches with access ports and assigned VLANs. Connect the hosts to server-1 and enable Inter-VLAN routing between the switches.

Figure 3-13 Lab Topology

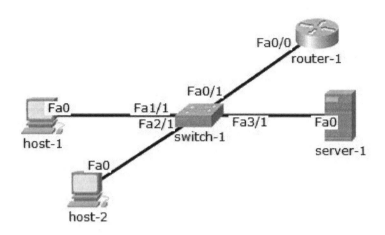

Lab Configuration

Start Packet Tracer File: **Lab 3-13 Inter-VLAN Routing**

Switch-1

Click on the *switch-1* icon and select the *CLI* folder. Hit the <enter> key for user mode prompt (>).

Step 1: Enter global configuration mode

> switch-1 > **enable** <enter>
> Password: **cisconet** <enter>
> switch-1# **configure terminal** <enter>

Step 2: Configure VLAN 10, VLAN 11 and VLAN 12

> switch-1(config)# **vlan 10** <enter>
> switch-1(config-vlan)# **vlan 11** <enter>
> switch-1(config-vlan)# **vlan 12** <enter>
> switch-1(config-vlan)# **exit** <enter>

Step 3: Configure interface Fa1/1 as an access port for host-1 and assign to VLAN 10

> switch-1(config)# **interface fastethernet1/1** <enter>
> switch-1(config-if)# **switchport mode access** <enter>
> switch-1(config-if)# **switchport access vlan 10** <enter>

Step 4: Configure interface Fa2/1 as an access port for host-2 and assign to VLAN 11

    switch-1(config)# **interface fastethernet2/1** <enter>
    switch-1(config-if)# **switchport mode access** <enter>
    switch-1(config-if)# **switchport access vlan 11** <enter>

Step 5: Configure interface Fa3/1 as an access port for server-1 and assign to VLAN 12

    switch-1(config)# **interface fastethernet3/1** <enter>
    switch-1(config-if)# **switchport mode access** <enter>
    switch-1(config-if)# **switchport access vlan 12** <enter>

Step 6: Configure interface Fa0/1 as a trunk

    switch-1(config)# **interface fastethernet0/1** <enter>
    switch-1(config-if)# **description uplink to router-1** <enter>
    switch-1(config-if)# **switchport mode trunk** <enter>

Step 7: Assign native VLAN 99 and only allow VLAN 10, 11 and 12 across the trunk

    switch-1(config-if)# **switchport trunk native vlan 999** <enter>
    switch-1(config-if)# **switchport trunk allowed vlan 10-12** <enter>
    switch-1(config-if)# **end** <enter>
    switch-1# **copy running-config startup-config** <enter>

Router-1

Click on the *router-1* icon and select the *CLI* folder. Hit the <enter> key for user mode prompt (>).

Step 8: Enter global configuration mode

    router-1 > **enable** <enter>
    Password: **cisconet** <enter>
    router-1# **configure terminal** <enter>

Step 9: Enable interface Fa0/0 with no IP address on router-1

    router-1(config)# **interface fastethernet0/0** <enter>
    router-1(config)# **description link to switch-1** <enter>
    router-1(config-if)# **no ip address** <enter>
    router-1(config-if)# **speed auto** <enter>
    router-1(config-if)# **duplex auto** <enter>
    router-1(config-if)# **no shutdown** <enter>
    router-1(config-if)# **exit** <enter>

Step 10: Configure subinterface Fa0/0.10 and assign to VLAN 10 subnet

    router-1(config)# **interface fastethernet0/0.10** <enter>
    router-1(config-subif)# **encapsulation dot1q 10** <enter>
    router-1(config-subif)# **ip address 192.168.10.254 255.255.255.0** <enter>

Step 11: Configure subinterface Fa0/0.11 and assign to VLAN 11 subnet

> router-1(config-subif)# **interface fastethernet0/0.11** <enter>
> router-1(config-subif)# **encapsulation dot1q 11** <enter>
> router-1(config-subif)# **ip address 192.168.11.254 255.255.255.0** <enter>

Step 12: Configure subinterface Fa0/0.12 and assign to VLAN 12 subnet

> router-1(config-subif)# **interface fastethernet0/0.12** <enter>
> router-1(config-subif)# **encapsulation dot1q 12** <enter>
> router-1(config-subif)# **ip address 192.168.12.254 255.255.255.0** <enter>
> router-1(config-subif)# **end** <enter>
> router-1# **copy running-config startup-config** <enter>

Step 13: <u>Verify Lab</u>

Confirm the configuration is correct on switch-1 and router-1

> switch-1# **show running-config** <enter>
>
> router-1# **show running-config** <enter>

Confirm all interfaces are operational (Resize *CLI* box to the right)

> switch-1# **show vlan brief** <enter>
>
> switch-1# **show cdp neighbors** <enter>
>
> switch-1# **show interfaces trunk** <enter>
>
> router-1# **show ip interface brief** <enter>

Confirm the VLAN subnets are installed in the routing table of router-1

> router-1# **show ip route** <enter>
>
> C   192.168.10.0/24 is directly connected, FastEthernet0/0.10
> C   192.168.11.0/24 is directly connected, FastEthernet0/0.11
> C   192.168.12.0/24 is directly connected, FastEthernet0/0.12

Ping host-2 from host-1 to confirm Inter-VLAN routing between VLAN 10 and VLAN 11 is working.

> host-1: **c:\> ping 192.168.11.1** <enter>

Ping server-1 from host-1 to confirm Inter-VLAN routing between VLAN 10 and VLAN 12 is working.

> host-1: **c:\> ping 192.168.12.1** <enter>

Ping server-1 from host-2 to confirm Inter-VLAN routing between VLAN 11 and VLAN 12 is working.

> host-2: **c:\> ping 192.168.12.1** <enter>

Lab 3-14: eBGP Peering

Lab Summary: Configure external BGP (eBGP) peering between router-1 and router-2. In addition advertise directly connected routes to the BGP neighbor.

Figure 3-14 Lab Topology

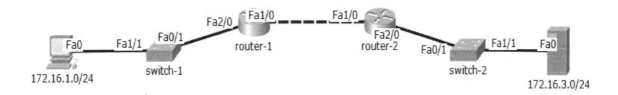

Lab Configuration

Start Packet Tracer File: **Lab 3-14 eBGP Peering**

Router-1

Click on the *router-1* icon and select the *CLI* folder. Hit the <enter> key for user mode prompt (>).

Step 1: Enter global configuration mode

    router-1 > **enable** <enter>
    Password: **cisconet** <enter>
    router-1# **configure terminal** <enter>

Step 2: Enable BGP routing and assign AS 65535

    router-1(config)# **router bgp 65535** <enter>

Step 3: Configure eBGP peering with neighbor assigned to AS 65534

    router-1(config-router)# **neighbor 192.168.1.2 remote-as 65534** <enter>

Step 4: Advertise host subnet to BGP peering neighbor

    router-1(config-router)# **network 172.16.1.0 mask 255.255.255.0** <enter>
    router-1(config-router)# **end** <enter> <enter>
    router-1# **copy running-config startup-config** <enter> <enter>

Router-2

Click on the *router-2* icon and select the *CLI* folder. Hit the <enter> key for user mode prompt (>).

Step 5: Enter global configuration mode

    router-2 > **enable** <enter>
    Password: **cisconet** <enter>
    router-2# **configure terminal** <enter>

Step 6: Enable BGP routing and assign AS 65534

router-2(config)# **router bgp 65534** <enter>

Step 7: Configure eBGP peering with neighbor assigned to AS 65535

router-2(config-router)# **neighbor 192.168.1.1 remote-as 65535** <enter> <enter>

Step 8: Advertise server-1 subnet to BGP peering neighbor

router-2(config-router)# **network 172.16.3.0 mask 255.255.255.0** <enter>
router-2(config-router)# **end** <enter> <enter>
router-2# **copy running-config startup-config** <enter> <enter>

Step 9: Verify Lab

Confirm the configuration is correct on router-1 and router-2

router-1# **show running-config** <enter>

router-2# **show running-config** <enter>

Confirm eBGP neighbors are in *Established* status

router-1# **show ip bgp neighbors** <enter>

BGP neighbor is 192.168.1.2, remote AS 65534, external link
BGP version 4, remote router ID 192.168.1.2
BGP state = Established, up for 00:00:17
Last read 00:00:17, last write 00:00:17, hold time is 180, keepalive interval is 60 seconds

Confirm the BGP routes in the routing table

router-1# **show ip bgp** <enter>

Network	Next Hop	Metric	LocPrf	Weight	Path
*> 172.16.1.0/24	0.0.0.0	0	0	32768	i
*> 172.16.3.0/24	192.168.1.2	0	0	0	65534 i

router-1# **show ip route** <enter>

router-2# **show ip bgp** <enter>

router-2# **show ip route** <enter>

Ping server-1 to verify routing is working across the network

router-1# **ping 172.16.3.1** <enter>

Lab Notes

BGP already advertises directly connected routes. The routes typically advertised are default, connected subnets and non-connected subnets. Static routes are required for any non-connected subnets where there is no IGP enabled. BGP only advertises routes already in the routing table.

4.0 IPv6 Addressing

Lab 4-1: Link-Local Addressing

Lab Summary: Enable IPv6 packet forwarding and automatic Link-local addressing on router interfaces

Figure 4-1 Lab Topology

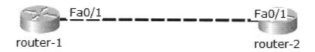

Lab Configuration

Start Packet Tracer File: **Lab 4-1 IPv6 Link-Local**

Click on the *router-1* icon and select the *CLI* folder. Hit the <enter> key for user mode prompt (>).

Step 1: Enter global configuration mode

 router-1 > **enable** <enter>
 Password: **cisconet** <enter>
 router-1# **configure terminal** <enter>

Router-1

Step 2: Enable IPv6 packet forwarding

 router-1(config)# **ipv6 unicast-routing** <enter>

Step 3: Configure interface Fa0/1 to automatically assign an IPv6 link-local address

 router-1(config)# **interface fastethernet0/1** <enter>
 router-1(config-if)# **description link to router-2** <enter>
 router-1(config-if)# **ipv6 enable** <enter>
 router-1(config-if)# **no shutdown** <enter> <enter>
 router-1(config-if)# **end** <enter> <enter>
 router-1# **copy running-config startup-config** <enter>

Router-2

Click on the *router-2* icon and select the *CLI* folder. Hit the <enter> key for user mode prompt (>).

Step 4: Enter global configuration mode

 router-2 > **enable** <enter>
 Password: **cisconet** <enter>
 router-2# **configure terminal** <enter>

Step 5: Enable IPv6 packet forwarding

router-2(config)# **ipv6 unicast-routing** <enter>

Step 6: Configure interface Fa0/1 to automatically assign an IPv6 link-local address

router-2(config)# **interface fastethernet0/1** <enter>
router-2(config-if)# **description link to router-1** <enter>
router-2(config-if)# **ipv6 enable** <enter>
router-2(config-if)# **no shutdown** <enter> <enter>
router-2(config-if)# **end** <enter> <enter>
router-2# **copy running-config startup-config** <enter>

Step 7: Verify Lab

Confirm the IPv6 configuration is correct and interfaces are enabled with an IPv6 link local address. The link-local addresses have a prefix of *FE80::* and are not installed in the routing table. All IPv6 interfaces are assigned a link-local address for connectivity purposes. The IOS command **show ipv6 interface fastethernet0/1** lists the operational status of the interface (up/up), IPv6 addressing and configured settings.

router-1# **show running-config** <enter>

router-1# **show ipv6 interface brief** <enter>

router-1# **show ipv6 interface fastethernet0/1** <enter>

router-2# **show running-config** <enter>

router-2# **show ipv6 interface brief** <enter>

router-2# **show ipv6 interface fastethernet0/1** <enter>

Lab 4-2: IPv6 Stateless Address Autoconfiguration (SLAAC)

Lab Summary: Enable IPv6 Stateless Address Autoconfiguration on all hosts connected to router-1.

Figure 4-2 Lab Topology

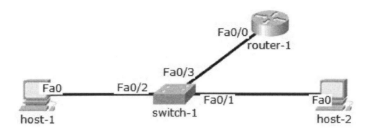

Lab Configuration

Start Packet Tracer File: **Lab 4-2 IPv6 SLAAC**

Router-1

Click on the *router-1* icon and select the *CLI* folder. Hit the <enter> key for user mode prompt (>).

Step 1: Enter global configuration mode

> router-1 > **enable** <enter>
> Password: **cisconet** <enter>
> router-1# **configure terminal** <enter>

Step 2: Enable IPv6 packet forwarding

> router-1(config)# **ipv6 unicast-routing** <enter>

Step 3: Configure an IPv6 address for interface Fa0/0

> router-1(config)# **interface fastethernet0/0** <enter>
> router-1(config-if)# **description link to switch-1** <enter>
> router-1(config-if)# **ipv6 address 2001:db8:3c4d:1::3/64** <enter>
> router-1(config-if)# **no shutdown** <enter> <enter>
> router-1(config-if)# **end** <enter> <enter>
> router-1# **copy running-config startup-config** <enter>

Step 4: Configure *Host-1* for IPv6 Autoconfiguration

- Click on the *host-1* icon
- Select *Config* folder
- Type 192.168.1.3 in IPv4 Gateway Address box
- Select Auto Config option for Gateway/DNS IPv6
- Select *FastEthernet0* button on the left
- Type 192.168.1.1 in Static IP Address box

- Click in Subnet Mask box to verify 255.255.255.0 appears
- Exit from host-1 configuration

Step 5: Configure *Host-2* for IPv6 Autoconfiguration

- Click on the *host-2* icon
- Select *Config* folder
- Type 192.168.1.3 in IPv4 Gateway Address box
- Select Auto Config option for Gateway/DNS IPv6
- Select *FastEthernet0* button on the left
- Type 192.168.1.2 in Static IP Address box
- Click in Subnet Mask box to verify 255.255.255.0 appears
- Exit from host-2 configuration

Step 6: Verify Lab

Confirm the IPv6 configuration is correct on router-1 and interface Fa0/0 is enabled with IPv6 addressing. Ping router-1 from host-1 to verify layer 3 connectivity (same subnet). In addition confirm all network connected devices are assigned a link-local address (FE80) and an IPv6 global unicast address with 2001::/64 prefix.

router-1# **show running-config** <enter>

router-1# **show ipv6 interface brief** <enter>

router-1# **show ipv6 interface fastethernet0/0** <enter>

host-1: **c:\> ping 2001:DB8:3C4D:1::3** <enter>

host-1: hover pointer over host-1 icon and verify IPv4/IPv6 addressing
host-1: **c:\> ipconfig /all** <enter>

host-2: hover pointer over host-2 icon and verify IPv4/IPv6 addressing
host-2: **c:\> ipconfig /all** <enter>

Lab 4-3: IPv6 Global Unicast Addressing

Lab Summary: Enable IPv6 packet forwarding between routers and configure IPv6 global unicast
static addresses on all LAN/WAN router interfaces.

Figure 4-3 Lab Topology

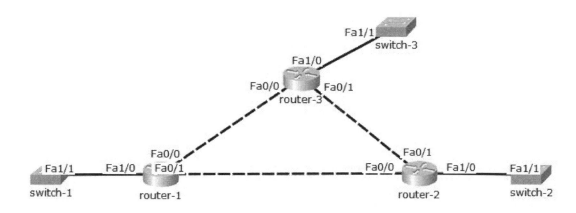

Lab Configuration

Start Packet Tracer File: **Lab 4-3 IPv6 Global Unicast**

Router-1

Click on the *router-1* icon and select the *CLI* folder. Hit the <enter> key for user mode prompt (>).

Step 1: Enter global configuration mode

> router-1 > **enable** <enter>
> Password: **cisconet** <enter>
> router-1# **configure terminal** <enter>

Step 2: Enable IPv6 packet forwarding

> router-1(config)# **ipv6 unicast-routing** <enter>

Step 3: Configure an IPv6 global unicast address on LAN interface Fa1/0

> router-1(config)# **interface fastethernet1/0** <enter>
> router-1(config-if)# **description link to switch-1** <enter>
> router-1(config-if)# **ipv6 address 2001:db8:3c4d:4::1/64** <enter>
> router-1(config-if)# **no shutdown** <enter> <enter>
> router-1(config-if)# **exit** <enter> <enter>

Step 4: Configure an IPv6 global unicast address on WAN interface Fa0/0

```
router-1(config)# interface fastethernet0/0 <enter>
router-1(config-if)# description link to router-3 <enter>
router-1(config-if)# ipv6 address 2001:db8:3c4d:1::1/64 <enter>
router-1(config-if)# no shutdown <enter> <enter>
router-1(config-if)# exit <enter> <enter>
```

Step 5: Configure an IPv6 global unicast address on WAN interface Fa0/1

```
router-1(config)# interface fastethernet0/1 <enter>
router-1(config-if)# description link to router-2 <enter>
router-1(config-if)# ipv6 address 2001:db8:3c4d:2::1/64 <enter>
router-1(config-if)# no shutdown <enter> <enter>
router-1(config-if)# end <enter> <enter>
router-1# copy running-config startup-config <enter>
```

Router-2

Click on the *router-2* icon and select the *CLI* folder. Hit the <enter> key for user mode prompt (>).

Step 6: Enter global configuration mode

```
router-2 > enable <enter>
Password: cisconet <enter>
router-2# configure terminal <enter>
```

Step 7: Enable IPv6 packet forwarding

```
router-2(config)# ipv6 unicast-routing <enter>
```

Step 8: Configure an IPv6 global unicast address on LAN interface Fa1/0

```
router-2(config)# interface fastethernet1/0 <enter>
router-2(config-if)# description link to switch-2 <enter>
router-2(config-if)# ipv6 address 2001:db8:3c4d:5::1/64 <enter>
router-2(config-if)# no shutdown <enter> <enter>
router-2(config-if)# exit <enter>
```

Step 9: Configure an IPv6 global unicast address on WAN interface Fa0/0

```
router-2(config)# interface fastethernet0/0 <enter>
router-2(config-if)# description link to router-1 <enter>
router-2(config-if)# ipv6 address 2001:db8:3c4d:2::2/64 <enter>
router-2(config-if)# no shutdown <enter> <enter>
router-2(config-if)# exit <enter>
```

Step 10: Configure an IPv6 global unicast address on WAN interface Fa0/1

> router-2(config)# **interface fastethernet0/1** <enter>
> router-2(config-if)# **description link to router-3** <enter>
> router-2(config-if)# **ipv6 address 2001:db8:3c4d:3::2/64** <enter>
> router-2(config-if)# **no shutdown** <enter>
> router-2(config-if)# **end** <enter>
> router-2# **copy running-config startup-config** <enter>

Router-3

Click on the *router-3* icon and select the *CLI* folder. Hit the <enter> key for user mode prompt (>).

Step 11: Enter global configuration mode

> router-3 > **enable** <enter>
> Password: **cisconet** <enter>
> router-3# **configure terminal** <enter>

Step 12: Enable IPv6 packet forwarding

> router-3(config)# **ipv6 unicast-routing** <enter>

Step 13: Configure an IPv6 global unicast address on LAN interface Fa1/0

> router-3(config)# **interface fastethernet1/0** <enter>
> router-3(config-if)# **description link to switch-3** <enter>
> router-3(config-if)# **ipv6 address 2001:db8:3c4d:6::1/64** <enter>
> router-3(config-if)# **no shutdown** <enter> <enter>
> router-3(config-if)# **exit** <enter>

Step 14: Configure an IPv6 global unicast address on WAN interface Fa0/0

> router-3(config)# **interface fastethernet0/0** <enter>
> router-3(config-if)# **description link to router-1** <enter>
> router-3(config-if)# **ipv6 address 2001:db8:3c4d:1::2/64** <enter>
> router-3(config-if)# **no shutdown** <enter> <enter>
> router-3(config-if)# **exit** <enter>

Step 15: Configure an IPv6 global unicast address on WAN interface Fa0/1

> router-3(config)# **interface fastethernet0/1** <enter>
> router-3(config-if)# **description link to router-2** <enter>
> router-3(config-if)# **ipv6 address 2001:db8:3c4d:3::1/64** <enter>
> router-3(config-if)# **no shutdown** <enter> <enter>
> router-3(config-if)# **end** <enter>
> router-3# **copy running-config startup-config** <enter>

Step 16: <u>Verify Lab</u>

Confirm the IPv6 configuration is correct and interfaces are operational (up/up) with the IPv6 static addressing assigned. All enabled interfaces are assigned a link-local address (FE80) and global unicast address (2001). In addition ping the IPv6 address of directly connected neighbor interfaces.

       router-1# **show running-config** <enter>

       router-1# **show ipv6 interface brief** <enter>

       router-1# **show ipv6 interface fastethernet0/0** <enter>

       router-1# **show ipv6 interface fastethernet0/1** <enter>

       router-1# **ping 2001:db8:3c4d:1::2** <enter>

       router-1# **ping 2001:db8:3c4d:2::2** <enter>

       router-2# **show running-config** <enter>

       router-2# **show ipv6 interface brief** <enter>

       router-2# **show ipv6 interface fastethernet0/0** <enter>

       router-2# **show ipv6 interface fastethernet0/1** <enter>

       router-2# **ping 2001:db8:3c4d:2::1** <enter>

       router-2# **ping 2001:db8:3c4d:3::1** <enter>

       router-3# **show running-config** <enter>

       router-3# **show ipv6 interface brief** <enter>

       router-3# **show ipv6 interface fastethernet0/0** <enter>

       router-3# **show ipv6 interface fastethernet0/1** <enter>

       router-3# **ping 2001:db8:3c4d:1::1** <enter>

       router-3# **ping 2001:db8:3c4d:3::2** <enter>

5.0 Network Troubleshooting

The network troubleshooting section is comprised of labs selected from various CCNA topics. The labs have errors for troubleshooting to restore network connectivity. The candidate will learn how to resolve network problems with a methodology for troubleshooting all layers of the OSI model.

Lab Conventions:

- Press the <enter> key and type **enable** to start or with idle devices (no enable password).
- Some show commands require you to resize the CLI window (drag right) when results are jumbled.
- The <arrow up> key is available to list all results for some show commands.
- Press *fast forward* button when starting lab and after configuration changes to speed convergence.

Troubleshooting Labs

- Lab 5-1: Interface Errors
- Lab 5-2: Trunking
- Lab 5-3: Static Routing
- Lab 5-4: EIGRP Neighbor Adjacency
- Lab 5-5: EIGRP K Values
- Lab 5-6: OSPF Timers
- Lab 5-7: Access Control Lists (ACL)
- Lab 5-8: Default Gateway
- Lab 5-9: DHCP Server
- Lab 5-10: PPP Authentication
- Lab 5-11 Port Security
- Lab 5-12: Inter-VLAN Routing
- Lab 5-13: Remote Management
- Lab 5-14: Traceroute
- Lab 5-15: Routing and Switching

Lab 5-1: Switch Interfaces

Incident Report: Single user reports performance and intermittent connectivity issues to server-1.

CCNA Topic: LAN Switching Technologies

Figure 5-1 Lab Topology

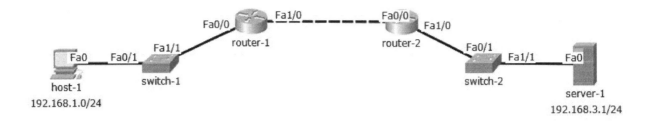

Start Packet Tracer File: **Lab 5-1 Switch Interfaces**

Troubleshooting Steps:

1. Ping from host-1 to server-1: **c:\> ping 192.168.3.1 (no)**
2. Verify the operational status of the switch-1 interface assigned to host-1:

    switch-1# show interfaces fastethernet0/1 (down/down)
3. Verify the operational status of the switch uplink interface to router-1:

    switch-1# show interfaces fastethernet1/1 (up/up)
4. Verify the interface configuration settings for Fa0/1: **switch-1# show running-config**
5. Select host-1 icon, *Config* folder, FastEthernet0 button to verify the duplex setting on Fa0.

Analysis

The **ping** from host-1 to server-1 verifies there is no connectivity from host-1 with *request timed out* errors. The next step is to verify the operational status of the switch-1 interface assigned to host-1 (Fa0/1). The **show interfaces** command verified the switch interface status is operational (down/down). That confirms there is no layer 2 connectivity from host-1. The **show running-config** command confirmed that interface Fa0/1 is manually configured with half-duplex setting. The duplex setting for host-1 interface Fa0 is configured as full-duplex. The current duplex setting on switch-1 is mismatched with the host network interface card. That is the causing layer 2 errors and no connectivity for host-1.

Resolution

The Cisco recommended best practice is to configure **auto/auto** for duplex and speed on all switch interfaces. That allows for auto-negotiation between host and switch or inter-switch connections.

    switch-1(config)# **interface fastethernet0/1** <enter>
    switch-1(config-if)# **duplex auto** <enter>
    switch-1(config-if)# **end** <enter>
    switch-1# **copy running-config startup-config** <enter>

Lab 5-2: Trunking

Incident Report: Host-1 cannot access any applications on server-1.

CCNA Topic: LAN Switching Technologies

Figure 5-2 Lab Topology

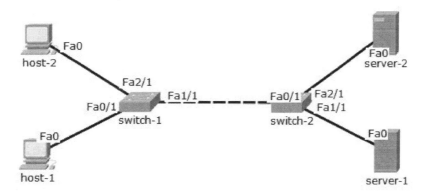

Start Packet Tracer File: **Lab 5-2 Trunking**

<u>Troubleshooting Steps:</u>

1. Verify that host-1 and server-1 are assigned to the same subnet by hovering over each icon.

2. Verify that host-2 and server-2 are assigned to the same subnet by hovering over each icon.

3. Ping from host-1 to server-1: **c:\> ping 192.168.1.2 (no)**

4. Verify the operational status of all switch-1 and switch-2 interfaces:

   switch-1# show ip interface brief
   switch-2# show ip interface brief

5. Find the MAC (physical) address of host-1 from the command prompt: **c:\> ipconfig /all**

6. Verify if the MAC address of host-1 is listed in the MAC address table:

   switch-1# show mac address-table (yes)

7. Confirm the VLAN assignment for host-1 (Fa0/1): **switch-1# show running-config**

8. Verify that VLAN 10 is active and assigned to Fa0/1 on switch-1: **switch-1# show vlan brief**

9. Confirm that server-1 (Fa1/1) is assigned to the same VLAN 10 as host-1:

   switch-2# show running-config

10. Verify that VLAN 10 is active and assigned to Fa1/1 on switch-2: **switch-2# show vlan brief**

11. Verify the operational status of the trunk: **switch-1# show interfaces trunk**

12. Verify the trunk configuration settings of both switches (interface, mode, vlans, native vlan):

    switch-1# **show running-config**
    switch-2# **show running-config**

Analysis

It was verified that host-1 and server-1 are assigned to 192.168.1.0/24 subnet. The **ping** from host-1 confirms there is no connectivity to server-1. There is no routing required when the **ping** is within the same subnet. The result of **show ip interface brief** commands confirm that switch-1 and switch-2 interfaces are all operational (up/up). There is layer 2 connectivity from host-1 and between the switches as well.

The results of **ipconfig /all** command list the MAC address of host-1 to verify if it is in the MAC address table. The **show mac address-table** command confirms the MAC address of host-1 is listed in the switch-1 table.

The next step is to verify the switch-1 interface of host-1 (Fa0/1) is assigned to VLAN 10 with **show running-config** command. The **show vlan brief** command confirms VLAN 1, 10 and 11 are active on switch-1. The same steps were repeated to verify the switch-2 interface of server-1 (Fa1/1) is assigned to VLAN 10 and is active.

The results of **show interfaces trunk** confirm the trunk is operational and trunk mode is desirable. In addition only VLAN 11 and VLAN 12 are allowed across the trunk. There is no VLAN 12 so it is a configuration error. Any traffic from VLAN 10 is not allowed and not forwarded across the trunk. The trunk settings are verified on each switch with **show running-config** to confirm they are incorrect.

Resolution

Configure the trunk interfaces on switch-1 (Fa1/1) and switch-2 (Fa0/1) to allow traffic from VLAN 10.

> switch-1(config)# **interface fastethernet1/1** <enter>
> switch-1(config-if)# **switchport trunk allowed vlan 10,11** <enter>
> switch-1(config-if)# **end** <enter>
> switch-1# **copy running-config startup-config** <enter>
>
> switch-2(config)# **interface fastethernet0/1** <enter>
> switch-2(config-if)# **switchport trunk allowed vlan 10,11** <enter>
> switch-2(config-if)# **end** <enter>
> switch-2# **copy running-config startup-config** <enter>

Lab Notes

There is **show interface switchport** command as well that provides operational status on switch ports.

Lab 5-3: Static Routing

Incident Report: Hosts on VLAN 12 of switch-1 cannot access a new server connected to switch-2.

CCNA Topic: Routing Technologies

Figure 5-3 Lab Topology

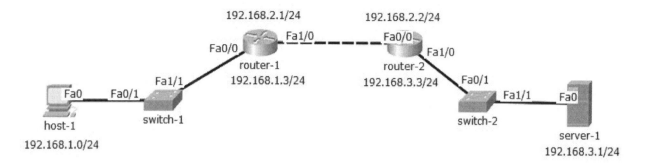

Start Packet Tracer File: **Lab 5-3 Static Routing**

Troubleshooting Steps

1. Ping from host-1 to router-1 interface Fa1/0: **c:\> ping 192.168.2.1 (yes)**
2. Ping from host-1 to router-2 interface Fa0/0: **c:\> ping 192.168.2.2 (yes)**
3. Ping from host-1 to the LAN interface of router-2: **c:\> ping 192.168.3.3 (no)**
4. Verify the route/s to server-1 installed in the routing table of router-1: **router-1# show ip route**
5. Verify the routing configuration of router-1: **router-1# show running-config**

Analysis

The first **ping** from host-1 to router-1 confirms layer 1 through layer 3 is working correctly to that point. The second **ping** confirms there is layer 3 connectivity and routing between host-1 and router-2. The third **ping** confirms there is a connectivity issue at layer 3 or higher between host-1 and server-1 subnets. Some of the typical causes of problems include routing and access control lists. Layer 3 connectivity only confirms packet forwarding between network devices on the same subnet. Packets that are forwarded correctly between external subnets confirms that routing is working.

The results of **show ip route** confirm there are no routes listed in the routing table of router-1 for the server-1 subnet (192.168.3.0/24). The configuration of router-1 was listed with **show running-config** to verify what if any routing is enabled. There is a static route that is forwarding traffic that is configured incorrectly. The static route is incorrectly forwarding traffic from hosts to 192.168.4.2 next hop address.

Resolution

Configure the static route so that the next hop address is router-2 interface Fa0/0 (192.168.2.2).

router-1(config)# **ip route 192.168.3.0 255.255.255.0 192.168.2.2** <enter>

Lab 5-4: EIGRP Neighbor Adjacency

Incident Report: All data center are unavailable from the branch office after a router upgrade.

CCNA Topic: Routing Technologies

Figure 5-4 Lab Topology

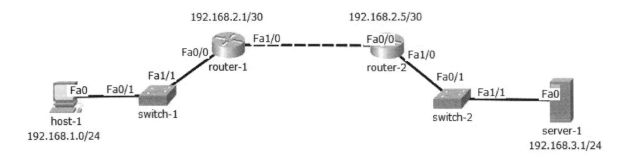

Start Packet Tracer File: **Lab 5-4 EIGRP Neighbor Adjacency**

Troubleshooting Steps:

1. Ping from host-1 to router-1 interface Fa1/0: **c:\> ping 192.168.2.1 (yes)**
2. Ping from host-1 to router-2: **c:\> ping 192.168.2.5 (no)**
3. Verify status of all L3 enabled interfaces on router-1: **router-1# show ip interface brief (up/up)**
4. Confirm router-1 has a route to router-2 for layer 3 reachability: **router-1# show ip route**
5. Ping from router-1 to the directly connected interface of router-2:

    router-2# ping 192.168.2.5 (no)
6. Verify the routing configuration on router-1: **router-1# show running-config**
7. Verify the routing configuration on router-2: **router-2# show running-config**
8. Verify there is EIGRP neighbor adjacency with router-2: **router-1: show ip eigrp neighbors**

Analysis

The first ping from host-1 to router-1 confirms there is layer 3 connectivity to that point. The second **ping** from host-1 to router-2 then isolates the problem to the link between routers. The operational status (up/up) and IP addressing of all layer 3 enabled interfaces on router-1 are confirmed with **show ip interface brief** command. There are two layer 3 interfaces enabled on router-1 with status and protocol **up/up** for each interface. It is key to know all the interfaces enabled when troubleshooting layer 3 issues.

The next step is to verify what routes are available in the routing table of router-1 to router-2. The results of **show ip route** confirm there is a directly connected route to router-2 (192.168.2.0/24) in the routing table of router-1. The third **ping** confirms there is no layer 3 connectivity to router-2. At this point the problem is pointing to some misconfiguration on either router.

The results of **show running-config** for router-1 confirm EIGRP is advertising 192.168.1.0/24 (host-1) and 192.168.2.0/24 (directly connected) subnets. The results of **show running-config** for router-2 confirm EIGRP is advertising 192.168.2.0/24 (directly connected) and 192.168.3.0 (server-1) subnets.

The directly connected interfaces of router-1 and router-2 however are on different subnets preventing EIGRP neighbor adjacency from forming. The directly connected physical interfaces on any point-to-point link must be assigned to the same subnet. The results of **show ip eigrp neighbors** confirms there is no neighbor adjacency with router-2 as a result.

The /30 subnet mask allows for only two host assignments per subnet. As a result router-2 (192.168.2.5) interface is in subnet 2.

> Subnet 1 = 192.168.2.0/30 - 192.168.2.3/30
> Subnet 2 = 192.168.2.4/30 – 192.168.2.7/30

Resolution

Assign router-2 interface Fa0/0 to the same subnet as router-1 interface Fa1/0.

> router-2(config)# **interface FastEthernet0/0** <enter>
> router-2(config-if)# **ip address 192.168.2.2 255.255.255.252** <enter>
> router-2(config-if)# **end** <enter>
> router-2# **copy running-config startup-config** <enter>

Lab Notes

EIGRP routes are advertised based on the global **network** commands under an EIGRP process (AS).

Lab 5-5: EIGRP K Values

Incident Report: All application on server-1 are unavailable after configuration changes to router-1.
CCNA Topic: Routing Technologies

Figure 5-5 Lab Topology

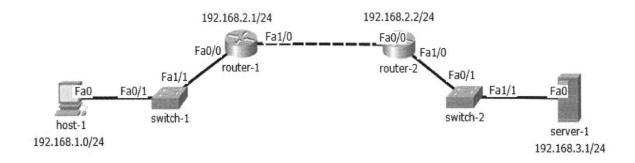

Start Packet Tracer File: **Lab 5-5 EIGRP K Values**

Troubleshooting Steps

1. Ping from host-1 to router-1 interface Fa1/0: **c:\> ping 192.168.2.1 (yes)**

2. Ping from host-1 to router-2 interface Fa0/0:: **c:\> ping 192.168.2.2 (no)**

3. Verify the status of all layer 3 interfaces on router-1: **router-1# show ip interface brief**

4. Verify the interface settings and any errors on router-1 interface Fa1/0:

   router-1# show interfaces fastethernet1/0

5. Verify the routes/s in the routing table of router-1 that are available to router-2:

   router-1# show ip route

6. Ping the directly connected neighbor interface of router-2 (Fa0/0):

   router-1# ping 192.168.2.2 (yes)

7. Verify the configuration of router-1 including routing and ACLs :

   router-1# show running-config

8. Verify the configuration of router-2 including routing and ACLs :

   router-2# show running-config

9. Verify EIGRP neighbor adjacency between router-1 and router-2:

   router-1# show ip eigrp neighbors

10. Verify the EIGRP K values configured on router-2: **router-2# show ip protocols**

11. Verify the EIGRP K values configured on router-1: **router-1# show ip protocols**

Analysis

The **ping** from host-1 to router-1 confirms there is layer 3 connectivity to router-1. The second **ping** from host-1 to router-2 confirms there is a connectivity issue between router-1 and router-2. The next step is to verify the status of all layer 3 interfaces on router-1. The results of **show ip interface brief** command lists all layer 3 enabled interfaces and assigned IP addressing on router-1. There is a layer 3 LAN interface and a WAN interface enabled and operational (up/up) on router-1. The results of **show interfaces** confirm there are no layer 2 interface errors.

The subnet assignment for all interfaces is a key aspect of any layer 3 troubleshooting. The next step is to verify what routes in the routing table of router-1 are available to router-2. In addition it is important to make note of the subnet mask (prefix length). The results of **show ip route** confirm there are directly connected routes only to router-2 and the host-1 subnet. The third **ping** confirms there is layer 3 connectivity to the directly connected interface of router-2 (Fa0/0). The **show running-config** command lists all configuration settings on both routers and confirms EIGRP is enabled. In addition the routers are on a common subnet with local subnets advertised. The results of **show ip eigrp neighbors** however confirm there is no neighbor adjacency formed between router-1 and router-2. There are a variety of configuration settings that could cause neighbor adjacency issues. The typical causes include either IP addressing or mismatched settings.

The **show ip protocols** command lists EIGRP global configuration settings for router-1. The same command issued on router-2 confirms it is configured with non-default K values. EIGRP neighbors cannot form an adjacency when there is a K value mismatch between neighbors. That prevents any routing of packets across the link and to server-1. In fact all routers assigned to the same EIGRP AS must have matching K values.

Resolution

Configure the K values to match on router-1 and router-2.

> router-1(config)# **router eigrp 1** <enter>
> router-1(config-router)# **metric weights 0 1 1 1 0 0** <enter>
> router-1(config-router)# **end** <enter>
> router-1# **copy running-config startup-config** <enter>

Lab Notes

The K values are assigned to EIGRP metrics and modified to affect routing path selection. The default K values include only bandwidth and delay metrics (010100) for EIGRP path selection.

> ToS = 0, Bandwidth = 1, Load = 0, Delay = 1, Reliability = 0, MTU = 0

Lab 5-6: OSPF Timers

Incident Report: Some applications are unavailable on server-1 after enabling OSPF on all routers.

CCNA Topic: Routing Technologies

Figure 5-6 Lab Topology

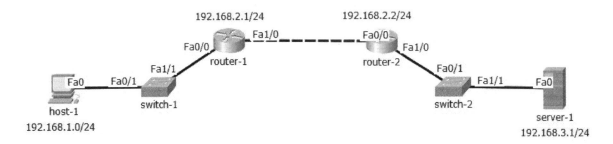

Start Packet Tracer File: **Lab 5-6 OSPF Timers**

Troubleshooting Steps

1. Ping from host-1 to router-1 interface Fa1/0: **c:\> ping 192.168.2.1 (yes)**
2. Ping from host-1 to router-2 interface Fa0/0: **c:\> ping 192.168.2.2 (no)**
3. Ping from router-1 to router-2 interface Fa0/0: **router-1# ping 192.168.2.2 (yes)**
4. Verify there is OSPF neighbor adjacency between router-1 and router-2:

      router-1# show ip ospf neighbor (no)
5. Verify the OSPF interface settings for router-1 interface Fa1/0:

      router-1# show ip ospf interface FastEthernet1/0

> operational status = up/up
> IP address: 192.168.2.1/24
> area 0
> network type: broadcast
> process ID 1
> timers: hello (1), dead (40) wait (40)

6. Verify the OSPF interface settings for router-2 interface Fa0/0:

      router-2# show ip ospf interface FastEthernet0/0

> operational status = up/up
> IP address: 192.168.2.2/24
> area 0
> network type: broadcast
> process ID 1
> timers: hello (10), dead (40) wait (40)

7. Verify the OSPF global and interface settings for router-1:

> router-1# **show running-config**
> router-2# **show running-config**

Analysis

Determining what has changed is a key aspect of any effective and efficient troubleshooting. In this lab we know OSPF routing was enabled on the routers and now server-1 is not available. Start with confirming layer 3 connectivity to router-1. The first **ping** confirms there is layer 3 connectivity from host-1 to server-1 and gateway addressing is correct. The second **ping** confirm there is no connectivity from host-1 to router-2. That isolates the problem to the link between router-1 and router-2. The typical causes are often hardware, routing misconfigurations or packet filtering with ACLs. The third **ping** confirms there is layer 3 connectivity between router-1 and router-2 (same subnet).

The next step is to confirm there is OSPF neighbor adjacency between the routers. The results of **show ip ospf neighbor** confirm there is no OSPF neighbor adjacency between router-1 and router-2. The results of **show ip ospf interface** command list the operational status and various OSPF settings of the directly connected router interfaces. There is a mismatch between the hello timer on router-1 and router-2. The hello timer is configured for 1 second on router-1 while router-2 has the default hello timer of 10 seconds. OSPF neighbor adjacencies won't form when there are timer mismatches. The OSPF interface settings for both routers are verified as well with the **show running-config** command.

Resolution

Delete the hello timer configuration on router-1 interface Fa1/0 or configure the same statement on router-2 interface Fa0/0. That will enable OSPF neighbor adjacency to form and exchange of routing updates for reachability to server-1. The following IOS commands delete the hello interval statement from router-1 interface Fa1/0.

> router-1(config)# **interface fastethernet1/0** <enter>
> router-1(config-if)# **no ip ospf hello-interval 1** <enter>
> router-1(config-if)# **end** <enter>
> router-1# **copy running-config startup-config** <enter>

Lab Notes

Mismatches are a common issue with OSPF neighbor connectivity. The neighbor link must match for area assigned, timers, MTU and network type. OSPF advertises routes based on enabled interfaces on a router that are within the range specified by the **network area** command. The area number designates the area where routes are advertised for the interfaces. The **network area** command is configured as an OSPF global command.

Lab 5-7: Access Control Lists (ACL)

Incident Report: All hosts assigned to VLAN 12 have no access to web-based applications on server-1.

CCNA Topic: Infrastructure Security

Figure 5-7 Lab Topology

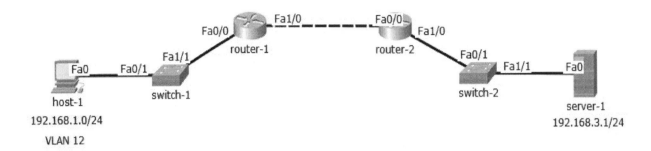

Start Packet Tracer File: **Lab 5-7 Access Control Lists**

Troubleshooting Steps

1. Ping from host-1 to server-1: **c:\> ping 192.168.3.1 (yes)**

2. Start an FTP session from the host to server-1 and confirm it is web-based applications only:

   > **c:\> ftp 192.168.3.1 (yes)**
   > username: *cisco*
   > password: *cisco*

   ftp > quit

3. Verify any access control lists (ACL) configured on router-1: **router-1# show access-lists**

4. Verify the current configuration on router-1: **router-1# show running-config**

Analysis

The **ping** confirms there is layer 3 connectivity from hosts on VLAN 12 to server-1. The next step is to verify it is an application layer problem. The FTP session worked fine and isolates the problem to the application layer. The most probable cause is some application layer filtering of web-based (HTTP) traffic from hosts assigned to VLAN 12. The filtering could include firewalls, proxy servers or access control lists. The topology shows there are only two routers and that is where ACLs are configured to filter traffic.

The traffic filter would require an extended access list typically deployed near the source (hosts). The **show access-lists** command confirms there is an ACL denying HTTP (www) traffic from subnet 192.168.1.0/24 (VLAN 12) to server-1. The **show running-config** command confirms ACL 100 is denying HTTP traffic to server-1 for that subnet. In addition the ACL is applied inbound on router-1 interface Fa0/0.

Resolution

Delete ACL 100 or remove it from router-1 interface Fa0/0 to allow VLAN 12 hosts access to all web-based applications on server-1

     router-1(config)# **interface fastethernet0/0** <enter>
     router-1(config-if)# **no ip access-group 100 in** <enter>
     router-1(config-if)# **end** <enter>
     router-1# **copy running-config startup-config** <enter>

Lab 5-8: Default Gateway

Incident Report: Branch employees can't access any data center applications after a new switch and router are installed.

CCNA Topic: Routing Technologies

Figure 5-8 Lab Topology

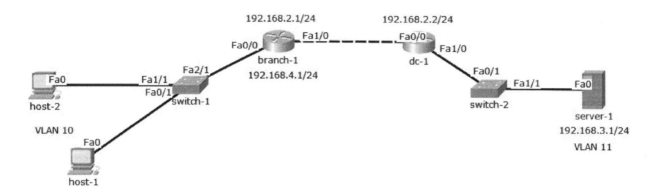

Start Packet Tracer File: **Lab 5-8 Default Gateway**

Troubleshooting Steps

1. Ping from branch-1 to server-1: **router-1# ping 192.168.3.1 (yes)**
2. Ping from host-1 to branch-1 interface Fa1/0: **c:\> ping 192.168.2.1 (no)**
3. Ping from host-1 to branch-1 interface Fa0/0: **c:\> ping 192.168.4.1 (no)**
4. Verify the operational status of the switch-1 interface assigned to host-1:

    switch-1# show interfaces fastethernet0/1 (up/up)

5. Verify the operational status of the switch-1 uplink interface to router-1:

    switch-1# show interfaces fastethernet2/1 (up/up)

6. Verify all switch-1 interfaces are in the same VLAN: **show vlan brief (yes)**
7. Verify the IP address and subnet assigned to host-1: **hover pointer over host-1 icon**

Analysis

The first **ping** confirms there is connectivity from the branch router to server-1 and the problem is isolated to the branch office inside network. The second **ping** results confirm there is no layer 3 connectivity between host-1 and branch-1 WAN interface. The third **ping** results confirm there is no layer 3 connectivity to the default gateway for host-1. The results of **show interfaces** commands verify there is layer 2 connectivity between host-1 and branch-1. The **show vlan brief** command verifies that VLAN 10 is active and all switch-1 interfaces are assigned to VLAN 10.

The next step is to verify the subnet assignment for all devices on the branch office inside network. The hosts and router-1 LAN interface must be assigned to the same subnet. It was noted after hovering pointer over host-1 that it is assigned 192.168.1.1/24 and a default gateway of 192.168.1.3/24. In addition host-2 is assigned 192.168.1.2/24 and a default gateway of 192.168.1.3/24. The LAN interface of router-1 is configured as 192.168.4.1/24 (Fa0/0). That confirms host-1 (192.168.1.0) and router-1 LAN interface (192.168.4.0) are not on the same subnet.

Resolution

Configure the LAN interface of router-1 interface Fa0/0 to 192.168.1.3/24

```
branch-1(config)# interface FastEthernet0/0 <enter>
branch-1(config-if)# ip address 192.168.1.3 255.255.255.0 <enter>
branch-1(config-if)# end <enter>
branch-1# copy running-config startup-config <enter>
```

Lab 5-9: DHCP Server

Incident Report: Host-1 cannot access any network applications at the data center.

CCNA Topic: Infrastructure Services

Figure 5-9 Lab Topology

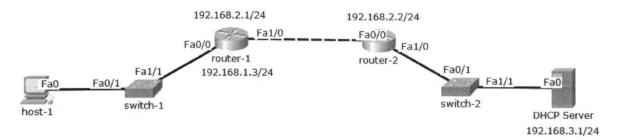

Start Packet Tracer File: **Lab 5-9 DHCP Server**

Troubleshooting Steps:

1. Ping from host-1 to router-1 interface Fa1/0: **c:\> ping 192.168.2.1 (no)**
2. Ping from host-1 to router-1 interface Fa0/0 (default gateway): **c:\> ping 192.168.1.3 (no)**
3. Verify the operational status of the switch-1 interface assigned to host-1:

   switch-1# show interfaces fastethernet0/1 (up/up)
4. Verify that all switch-1 ports are assigned to the same VLAN:

   switch-1# **show vlan brief**
5. Verify all IP address settings are correct on host-1: **c:\> ipconfig /all (none)**
6. Verify host-1 is enabled for DHCP: **select host-1 icon, select** *Config* **folder (yes)**
7. Ping the DHCP server from router-1 to verify reachability: **router-1# 192.168.3.1 (yes)**

Analysis

The first **ping** from host-1 to router-1 interface Fa1/0 confirms there is no layer 3 connectivity to that point. The second **ping** confirms there is no layer 3 connectivity at all from host-1 to router-1. The **show interfaces** command confirms the switch port assigned to host-1 (Fa0/1) is operational (up/up). That verifies there is layer 1 and layer 2 connectivity from host-1 to switch-1. In addition the interface settings are full duplex and 100 Mbps speed. The results of **show vlan brief** confirm VLAN 10 is active and assigned to both interfaces on switch-1.

The next step is to confirm host-1 is in the same subnet as the default gateway (router-1 interface Fa0/0) and configured with that gateway address. The results of the host command **ipconfig /all** confirm there is no IP addressing configured on host-1. In addition the DHCP feature is currently enabled in the *Config* folder. There is an IP address assigned by the host (169.254.0.0/16) however it is an IPv4 Link-local address (APIPA) and only supports same subnet (VLAN) connectivity. The DHCP server possibly did not respond to a request from host-1 for IP address settings. The **ping** from router-1 to the DHCP server verifies there is layer 3 reachability. The problem is with the configuration and/or operation of the DHCP server.

<u>Resolution</u>

The best approach is to send a new request to the DHCP server by selecting the host-1 *Desktop* folder, then *Command Prompt* of host-1. Examine the DHCP server for possible configuration errors if the request does not fix the issue.

> host-1: **c:\> ipconfig /release** <enter>
> host-1: **c:\> ipconfig /renew** <enter>

Lab 5-10: PPP Authentication

Incident Report: There is no connectivity from the branch office to the data center.

CCNA Topic: WAN Technologies

Figure 5-10 Lab Topology

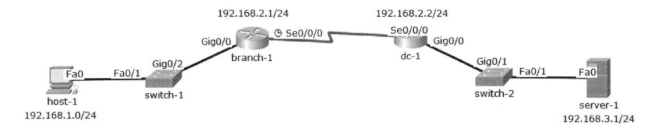

Start Packet Tracer File: **Lab 5-10 PPP Authentication**

Troubleshooting Steps:

1. Ping from host-1 to branch-1 interface Serial0/0/0: **c:\> ping 192.168.2.1 (no)**
2. Verify the operational status of router-1 interface Serial0/0/0:

    branch-1# show interfaces serial0/0/0 (up/down)

3. Verify PPP encapsulation is configured on both routers:

    branch-1# show interfaces serial0/0/0
    dc-1# show interfaces serial0/0/0

4. Verify the configuration of branch-1 interface Serial0/0/0: **branch-1# show running-config**
5. Verify the configuration of dc-1 interface Serial0/0/0: **dc-1# show running-config**

Analysis

The **ping** from host-1 to the serial0/0/0 (WAN) interface of branch-1 confirms there is no layer 3 connectivity to local branch-1 router. The results of **show interfaces serial0/0** confirm that line protocol is down (layer 2) for the branch-1 serial0/0/0 interface (up/down). Layer 3 connectivity is not available when layer 2 is not working correctly. The typical causes of layer 2 problems on a WAN interface include encapsulation, clocking and password mismatches.

The **show interfaces** command further verified there is an encapsulation mismatch between the routers. The branch-1 router is configured with PPP encapsulation while dc-1 is configured with HDLC. In addition the LCP status was closed on both serial interfaces for the PPP link confirming there is no layer 2 connectivity. The configuration settings are listed on both routers with the **show running-config** command. The results confirm the default HDLC encapsulation is configured on the serial interface of dc-1 instead of PPP encapsulation.

<u>Resolution</u>

Configure the encapsulation type to PPP on dc-1 interface Serial0/0/0.

dc-1(config)# **interface serial0/0/0** <enter>
dc-1(config-if)# **encapsulation ppp** <enter>
dc-1(config-if)# **end** <enter>
dc-1# **copy running-config startup-config** <enter>

Lab 5-11 Port Security

Incident Report: Host-1 cannot access any applications on server-1

CCNA Topic: LAN Switching Technologies

Figure 5-11 Lab Topology

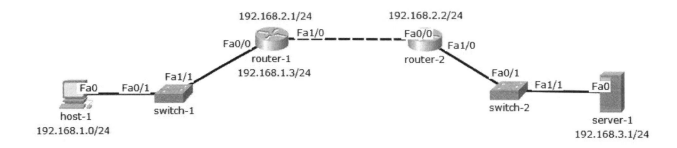

Start Packet Tracer File: **Lab 5-11 Port Security**

Troubleshooting Steps:

1. Confirm the operational status of the switch-1 interface assigned to host-1 (Fa0/1).

    switch-1# show interfaces fastethernet0/1 (up/up)

2. Ping from host-1 to router-1 interface Fa1/0: **c:\> ping 192.168.2.1 (no)**

3. Ping from host-1 to router-1 interface Fa0/0 (default gateway): **c:\> ping 192.168.1.3 (no)**

4. Verify the operational status of the switch-1 interface assigned to host-1 (Fa0/1):

    switch-1# show interfaces fastethernet0/1 (down/down)

5. Verify the operational status of the switch-1 uplink interface to router-1 (Fa1/1):

    switch-1# show interfaces fastethernet1/1 (up/up).

6. Verify the port security status for switch-1 interface Fa0/1:

    switch-1# show port-security interface fastethernet0/1

7. Verify the configuration settings for interface Fa0/1: **switch-1# show running-config**

8. Verify the MAC (physical) address assigned to host-1: **c:\> ipconfig /all**

Analysis

The lab starts with confirming the operational status of switch-1 interface Fa0/1 assigned to host-1 is *up/up*. The first **ping** result confirms there is no layer 3 connectivity from host-1 to the WAN interface of router-1 (Fa1/0). The second **ping** confirms there is no layer 3 connectivity at all from host-1 to router-1. The operational status of switch port Fa0/1 assigned to host-1 is confirmed with **show interfaces fastethernet0/1** as *down/down (err-disabled)*. The interface status of Fa0/1 changed to down after sending the ping from host-1.

The operational status of the switch uplink interface Fa1/1 to router-1 is confirmed with **show interfaces fastethernet1/1** as *up/up*. The port security operational status of interface Fa0/1 is then verified with **show port-security interface fastethernet0/1.** The results from that command confirm switch port Fa0/1 is in secure-shutdown mode. In addition there is one configured MAC address assigned to the switch port. The **show running-config** command lists the port security interface configuration settings. There is a static MAC address 0000.1234.5678 configured on switch port Fa0/1. The switch will only permit the host with that MAC address to forward packets ingress on that switch interface. The results of **ipconfig /all** confirm host-1 is not assigned that MAC address and as a result cannot forward packets to that switch interface.

Resolution

Remove the static MAC address configured on switch-1 interface Fa0/1 and power cycle the switch.

```
switch-1(config)# interface FastEthernet0/1 <enter>
switch-1(config-if)# no switchport port-security mac-address 0000.1234.5678 <enter>
switch-1(config-if)# end <enter>
switch-1# copy running-config startup-config <enter>
```

Lab 5-12: Router on a Stick

Incident Report: Hosts on VLAN 10 cannot access any applications on server-1 (VLAN 12)

CCNA Topic: Routing Technologies

Figure 5-12 Lab Topology

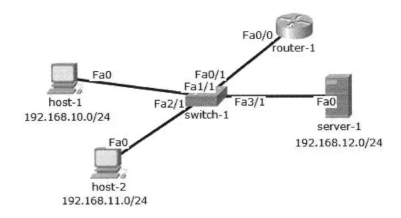

Start Packet Tracer File: **Lab 5-12 Router on a Stick**

Troubleshooting Steps

1. Ping from host-1 to router-1 subinterface for VLAN 10: **c:\> ping 192.168.10.254 [no]**
2. Ping from host-1 to router-1 subinterface for VLAN 11: **c:\> ping 192.168.11.254 [no]**
3. Ping from host-1 to router-1 subinterface for VLAN 12: **c:\> ping 192.168.12.254 [no]**
4. Ping from host-2 (VLAN 11) to server-1 (VLAN 12): **c:\> ping 192.168.12.1 [yes]**
5. Verify the trunk between switch-1 and router-1 is operational: **switch-1# show interfaces trunk**
6. Verify the IP address and subnet assigned to host-1: **c:\> ipconfig /all**
7. Verify the Inter-VLAN configuration settings on router-1: **router-1# show running-config**
8. Verify the subnets for VLAN 10, 11 and 12 in the routing table: **router-1# show ip route**

Analysis

The **ping** to each router subinterface from host-1 confirms there is no layer 3 connectivity from VLAN 10 to router-1 or any external VLAN (subnet). The fourth **ping** from host-2 to server-1 confirm server-1 is operational and Inter-VLAN routing is working correctly between VLAN 11 and VLAN 12.

The next step is to verify the trunk is operational between switch-1 and router-1 with **show interfaces trunk** command. The status column shows as *Trunking* on switch-1 interface Fa0/1 confirming it is working correctly there is layer 2 connectivity. In addition the trunk is configured to allow VLAN 10, VLAN 11 and VLAN 12.

At this point the problem is at layer 3 or higher and could include IP addressing and/or routing. The **ipconfig /all** command verifies host-1 is assigned to 192.168.10.1/24. That confirms as well that the subnet for VLAN 10 is 192.168.10.0/24.

The show **running-config** command on router-1 confirms subinterface Fa0/0.10 configured for VLAN 10 is assigned 192.168.9.254/24 address. The subinterface Fa0/0.10 for router-1 is configured with the wrong subnet (192.168.9.0/24). The result of **show ip route** confirm VLAN 10 subnet (192.168.10.0/24) is not installed in the routing table. Instead there is a route to 192.168.9.0/24 installed along with 192.168.11.0/24 and 192.168.12.0/24.

Resolution

Assign the IP address for subinterface Fa0/0.10 (VLAN 10) on router-1 to 192.168.10.254 address. That will enable Inter-VLAN routing from VLAN 10 (192.168.10.0) to VLAN 11 (192.168.11.0) and VLAN 12 (192.168.12.0).

router-1(config)# **interface FastEthernet0/0.10** <enter>
router-1(config-subif)# **ip address 192.168.10.254 255.255.255.0** <enter>
router-1(config-subif)# **end** <enter>
router-1# **copy running-config startup-config** <enter>

Lab 5-13: Remote Management

Incident Report: There is no remote management access available to switch-2.

CCNA Topic: Infrastructure Management

Figure 5-13 Lab Topology

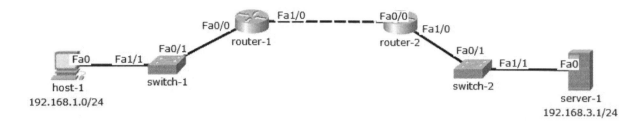

Start Packet Tracer File: **Lab 5-13 Remote Management**

Troubleshooting Steps

1. Ping from host-1 to server-1: **c:\> ping 192.168.3.1 (yes)**

2. List the running configuration on switch-2 and verify the following:

   switch-2# show running-config

3. Verify that VTY lines 0 4 are enabled with password and login: **(yes)**

   line vty 0 4
   password cisco
   login

4. Verify there is an enable password configured *(no)*

   enable password cisconet

5. Verify the default gateway address is 192.168.1.3 **(yes)**

   ip default-gateway 192.168.3.3

6. Verify the management VLAN interface *(no)*

   interface vlan 10
   ip address 192.168.3.255 255.255.255.0

Analysis

The **ping** results confirm there is layer 3 connectivity between host-1 and server-1. In addition it confirms that routing is working correctly to server-1 subnet (192.168.3.0/24). The results of **show running-config** confirm there is no enable password or layer 3 management interface (SVI) configured on switch-2. The enable password is required for Telnet/SSH remote access when there is no username and password configured (local authentication) with privilege level 15. The management VLAN (SVI) is required as well to advertise an IP address.

<u>Resolution</u>

Configure an enable password and management VLAN SVI on switch-2 with IP address 192.168.3.255/24 for management traffic.

> switch-2(config)# **enable password cisconet** <enter>
> switch-2(config)# **interface vlan 10** <enter>
> switch-2(config-if)# **ip address 192.168.3.255 255.255.255.0** <enter>
> switch-2(config-if)# **no shutdown** <enter>
> switch-2(config-if)# **end** <enter>
> switch-2# **copy running-config startup-config** <enter>

Lab 5-14: Traceroute

Incident Report: Intermittent degraded performance across WAN to applications at data center

CCNA Topic: Infrastructure Management

Figure 5-14 Lab Topology

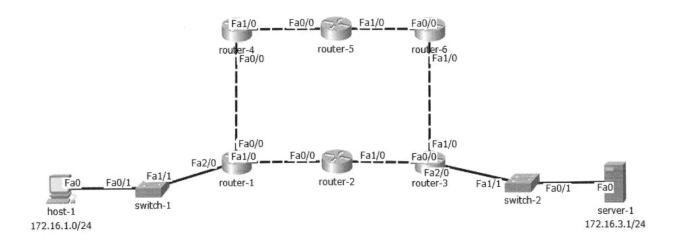

Start Packet Tracer File: **Lab 5-14 Traceroute**

Troubleshooting Steps:

1. Ping from host-1 to server-1: **c:\> ping 192.168.3.1 (yes)**
2. Verify there are no interface errors on the enabled switch-1 interfaces:

    switch-1# show interfaces fastethernet0/1
    switch-1# show interfaces fastethernet1/1

3. Verify there are no interface errors on the enabled switch-2 interfaces:

    switch-2# show interfaces fastethernet0/1
    switch-2# show interfaces fastethernet1/1

4. Verify the routing path from host-1 to server-1 with traceroute

    c:\> tracert 192.168.3.1

5. Verify the route to server-1 (172.16.3.0/24) in in the routing table of router-1 (resize box to right)

    router-1# show ip route

6. Verify the route to server-1 (172.16.3.0/24) is in the routing table of router-2 (resize box to right)

    router-2# show ip route

7. Verify the status of all layer 3 enabled interfaces on router-2

    router-2# show ip interface brief

Analysis

The first **ping** results confirm there is layer 3 connectivity between host-1 and server-1. That verifies there is a route to server-1 as well. The **show interfaces** commands verify there are no errors on the switch interfaces and all are full-duplex mode. The results of **traceroute** command confirm there is suboptimal routing to server-1. The most direct route is to forward packets to server-1 is from router-1 -> router-2 -> router-3. Instead the packets are being routed around via router-4. The next step is to determine where that route is being learned from starting with router-1. The **show ip route** command on router-1 verifies the route to server-1 subnet (172.16.3.0/24) is available however is being advertised (learned) from router-4 and not router-2.

All routers are configured with the same bandwidth and default EIGRP settings. As a result the preferred route should be advertised from router-2 based on default EIGRP route metrics. The second **show ip route** verifies 172.16.3.0/24 is in the routing table of router-2 and learned from router-3. Results of **show ip interface brief** on router-2 confirm interface Fa0/0 on router-2 is administratively down. There are no EIGRP routes advertised to router-1 from router-2 as a result. It is a good idea as well to confirm that the EIGRP **network** statements are configured correctly on router-2 and the autonomous system (EIGRP process) number is the same for all routers.

c:\> **tracert 192.168.3.1**

Tracing route to 172.16.3.1 over a maximum of 30 hops:

1	0 ms	19 ms	12 ms	172.16.1.2
2	29 ms	18 ms	24 ms	192.168.3.2
3	30 ms	24 ms	20 ms	192.168.4.2
4	15 ms	21 ms	30 ms	192.168.5.2
5	35 ms	35 ms	48 ms	192.168.6.2
6	*	42 ms	45 ms	172.16.3.1

Trace complete.

Resolution

Configure no shutdown on router-2 interface Fa0/0 to enable the interface.

> router-2(config)# **interface fastethernet0/0** <enter>
> router-2(config-if)# **no shutdown** <enter>
> router-2(config-if)# **end** <enter>
> router-2# **copy running-config startup-config** <enter>

Confirm that optimal routing exists from host-1 and/or router-1 to server-1 with the following commands:

> router-1# **traceroute 172.16.3.1** <enter>
> host-1: **c:\> tracert 172.16.3.1** <enter>

Lab 5-15: Routing and Switching

Incident Report: There is no network access from any location to the data center servers. In addition hosts cannot access web applications on server-1.

CCNA Topic: Routing and Switching Technologies

Figure 5-15 Lab Topology

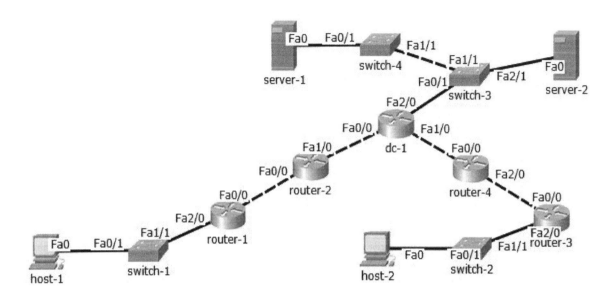

Start Packet Tracer File: **Lab 5-15 Routing and Switching**

Lab Strategy

There are no troubleshooting steps provided with this lab. The following strategy however will provide some guidance on how to proceed.

1. There are seven configuration errors to find and resolve.

2. CLI to all network devices and list the running configuration

3. Make a list of all IP addressing assigned to devices

4. Note the IP address settings for hosts and servers

5. Select either host-1 or host-2 and get connectivity working from a single location first

6. **Ping** from host to default gateway first and proceed forward

7. **Tracert** from host and determine where the routing problem is occurring

8. CLI to each network device and list running-configuration to identify any errors

9. Run show commands to verify layer 2 and layer 3 connectivity from each device

Analysis

The **ping** from host-1 and host-2 to server-1 and server-2 will verify all the issues are all resolved and the lab is working correctly.

> host-1: **c:\> ping 172.16.3.1** <enter>
> host-1: **c:\> ping 172.16.3.2** <enter>
> host-2: **c:\> ping 172.16.3.1** <enter>
> host-2: **c:\> ping 172.16.3.2** <enter>
> host-1: **http://172.16.3.1** <enter>
> host-2: **http://172.16.3.1** <enter>

Resolution

Email: ccna@cisconetsolutions.com for the correct steps to resolve all network problems as well.

Lab Notes

The are two different commands for doing a traceroute based on the network device. The host command line is **tracert.** The IOS command for Cisco routers and switches is **traceroute**.

The following are some show commands available for troubleshooting purposes:

- show running-config
- show vlan brief
- show ip interface brief
- show cdp neighbor
- show ip interfaces [interface]
- show interfaces trunk
- show ip route
- show ip ospf neighbor
- show ip eigrp neighbors

CCNA v3 Routing
and Switching

CCNA Routing and Switching 200-125 is a study guide for prospective CCNA v3 candidates. Cisco CCNA 200-125 is a single test option that includes both ICND1 100-105 and ICND2 200-105. There are significant changes made to the new CCNA curriculum. The study guide includes all new and updated CCNA 200-125 exam topics.

The book is comprised of 600+ questions and answers designed as a certification course with seven modules. The questions include detailed answers for all CCNA v3 exam topics. Some of the new CCNA topics covered include IPv6 addressing, MPLS, MLPPP, PPPoE, GRE, QoS, eBGP, SDN, APIC-EM and wireless devices. In addition there is coverage of LLDP, switch chassis aggregation, port-based authentication and DHCP snooping. The question and answer format is an effective technique to prepare for certification.

- 600+ Questions and Answers
- Official CCNA 200-125 Curriculum
- Module 1: Network Fundamentals
- Module 2: LAN Switching Technologies
- Module 3: Routing Technologies
- Module 4: WAN Technologies
- Module 5: Infrastructure Services
- Module 6: Infrastructure Security
- Module 7: Infrastructure Management

Made in the USA
Middletown, DE
20 May 2017